THE ADDICTION EQUATION

What is Having a Dependency All About?

THE ADDICTION EQUATION

What is Having a Dependency All About?

Lambert Low
MBBS (Singapore), MRCPsych (UK)
MSc (Addiction Studies),Dip Acup, FAMS (Psychiatry)
Institute of Mental Health, Singapore

Sara Cheo
MBBS (Australia), MRCP (UK), MMed (Singapore)
Ng Teng Fong General Hospital, Singapore

NEW JERSEY · LONDON · SINGAPORE · GENEVA · BEIJING · SHANGHAI · TAIPEI · CHENNAI

Published by

World Scientific Publishing Co. Pte. Ltd.

5 Toh Tuck Link, Singapore 596224

USA office: 27 Warren Street, Suite 401-402, Hackensack, NJ 07601

UK office: 57 Shelton Street, Covent Garden, London WC2H 9HE

British Library Cataloguing-in-Publication Data
A catalogue record for this book is available from the British Library.

THE ADDICTION EQUATION
What is Having a Dependency All About?

ISBN 978-981-98-1099-4 (hardcover)
ISBN 978-981-98-1175-5 (paperback)
ISBN 978-981-98-1100-7 (ebook for institutions)
ISBN 978-981-98-1101-4 (ebook for individuals)

For any available supplementary material, please visit
https://www.worldscientific.com/worldscibooks/10.1142/14250#t=suppl

Typeset by Stallion Press
Email: enquiries@stallionpress.com

"Dr Low offers a fresh perspective on understanding addiction through an innovative mathematical model. Dr Low simplifies his clinical experience making complex neurobiological and psychological concepts accessible to all. The book provides practical strategies for managing addictions, from substance abuse to behavioural dependencies, while fostering empathy and compassion. A thought-provoking tool for clinicians, patients, and families, The Addiction Equation bridges science and practice, offering valuable insights into the severity and management of addiction in today's world."

A/Prof Daniel Fung
Chief Executive Officer, Institute of Mental Health
Adjunct Associate Professor,
Yong Loo Lin School of Medicine,
National University of Singapore
DUKE-NUS Medical School and
Lee Kong Chian School of Medicine
Nanyang Technological University

"This is a thought-provoking book which starts off with the use of a novel mathematical formula to stimulate thinking about the clinical factors that may interact and inter-relate in the context of addictive disorders. The author distills insights from his clinical experience, observations and readings and shares his understanding on theories behind addictions, its chronicity, newer domains such as digital addiction, and practical ways to manage addictions. It is an invaluable read for those who want

to better understand the nature of addictions as well as help those who suffer from such conditions."

Dr Sim Kang
Senior Consultant
Assistant Chairman Medical Board (Education)
Institute of Mental Health
Associate Professor, Yong Loo Lin School of Medicine,
National University of Singapore
Associate Professor, Lee Kong Chian School of Medicine,
Nanyang Technological University

"In 'The Addiction Equation', Dr Lambert Low aptly provides the reader a good summary of the concepts and theories behind addictions and puts forth a fresh and novel equation to help a person with addiction problem quantify the severity of the addiction. I commend this brilliant book to all who are striving to understand more about the topic of addiction. I thoroughly enjoyed reading it and have learned a lot and I strongly believe you will feel likewise."

Adj Assoc Prof Lee Cheng
Former Programme Director
National Addiction Management Services
Adjunct Assistant Professor,
Department of Psychological Medicine,
National University of Singapore
Adjunct Associate Professor,
Lee Kong Chian School of Medicine
Nanyang Technological University

someone battling addiction, or a family member seeking guidance. It's written in a clear and relatable way, with practical insights, case studies, and quizzes to deepen understanding."

Miss Michelle Cheo
Board Member, The Helping Hand

ABOUT THE AUTHORS

Dr Lambert Low is the current chief of the Addiction Medicine Department at the Institute of Mental Health and the current Chairperson of the Section of Addiction Psychiatry, under the College of Psychiatrists. He is a psychiatrist whose special interest is in helping patients with addictions and he has treated a whole range of addictive conditions, ranging from substance to behavioural addictions. He has been frequently quoted in media pertaining to addiction related topics in Singapore and he is also a council member with the Singapore Medical Association.

Dr Sara Cheo is currently a consultant at the department of Gastroenterology at Ng Teng Fong General Hospital. She is also a member of the Gastroenterological Society of Singapore. She completed her Gastroenterology residency training in Tan Tock Seng Hospital. The patients she

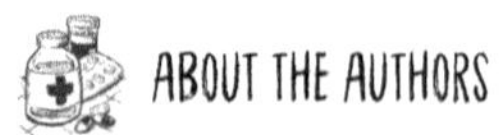

sees can have a range of gastroenterology-related problems, but her interest is in liver conditions, particularly fatty liver. She has articles published in scientific journals, including the American Journal of Gastroenterology.

FOREWORD

Dr. Lambert Low has brilliantly dissected a crucial and challenging issue of addiction into a concise and easy read for both practitioners and anyone seeking to understand addiction better. It includes quick references and quizzes to help the reader recall the key takeaways in each chapter. The Addiction Equation cleverly translates the concept of addiction with a mathematical equation, allowing us to relate to the various variables and contributing factors.

My heartfelt congratulations and sincere compliments to Dr. Lambert on this endeavor and for painstakingly writing and publishing this book, which I am confident will help and inspire many. I highly recommend diving into this insightful read!

Regards,
Patrick Tay Teck Guan
Chairman, Mental Health Board, NHG
Member of Parliament, Pioneer SMC

PREFACE

My name is Lambert, and I am a psychiatrist. This book is a culmination of my years of reading and working in the field of addictions, hopefully to provide much needed awareness to this very poorly understood illness called addictions. Many of the insights regarding addictions that are described in this book are distilled from my personal experiences and observations interacting and treating patients suffering from addictions, a journey that has spanned more than a decade. If some of these ideas don't resonate with you or if you find them unscientific, the truth is that there is still a lot we don't know and understand about addictions and it may well hold true that my observations and hypothesis still remains to be tested.

This book discusses what having an addiction means and provides a good summary of the concepts and theories behind addictions, putting forth a novel equation to help someone quantify the severity of any addiction.

For anyone who is suffering from an addiction to a concerned family member of friend, this book helps to understand and possibly provide helpful strategies to help manage the condition better. I also discuss novel addictions that might herald the beginning of a new age of addictions such as social media addiction.

It is my hope that after reading this book, you will not just have more compassion and empathy for anyone suffering with addictions, but also gain a better understanding of what it truly means to have an addiction.

This book is dedicated to my family, my wife Sara, who has supported me greatly in my journey as a psychiatrist, my children Isaac and Elizabeth who provide the nourishment to my soul every day, as well to my parents and parents-in-laws who provide me the stability I need to pursue this difficult line of work.

CONTENTS

About the Authors — ix

Foreword — xi

Preface — xiii

Chapter 1 — The Addiction Equation — 1

Chapter 2 — Do I have an addiction? — 19

Chapter 3 — Theories behind Addictions — 41

Chapter 4 — Addiction as a Chronic Illness — 57

Chapter 5 — New World Addictions-"Digital Heroin" — 75

Chapter 6 — Slow Things Down — 97

Chapter 7 — How to Manage an Addiction? — 111

Chapter 8 — Be Kind (to yourself and others) — 125

Chapter 9 — We are All in this Together — 143

Chapter 10 — Legal Aspects & The Addiction Equation Re-visited — 157

Chapter 11 — Alcohol and the Body — 175

Index — 195

1

THE ADDICTION EQUATION

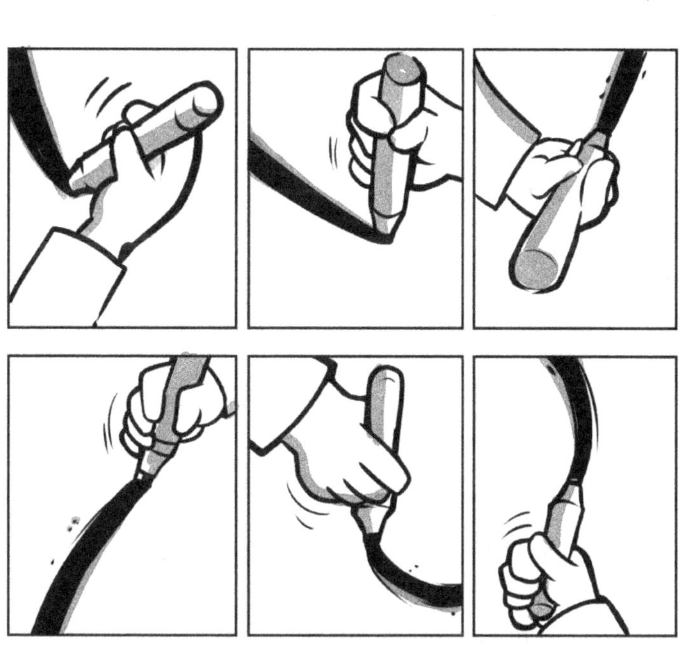

Not often does one conceptualize an Addiction in terms of a mathematical formula. In this book, I will seek to elaborate on this concept, a novel one and I will argue that the severity of any Addiction can be determined by one Mathematical Formula. Having practised in the field of Addictions for more than a decade as a psychiatrist, I am of the opinion that the severity of an addiction inevitably distils down to just a few variables. The Equation that I propose is as follows:

$$\text{Severity of Addiction} = \frac{(\text{Pleasure} + \text{Urge}) \times \text{Speed}^2}{\text{Control}}$$

The variables in this equation are defined as follows:

Pleasure-Degree or magnitude of positive sensations derived
Speed-Frequency of onset of a particular activity
Urge-The desire to use a particular substance or perform a particular activity
Control-Ability to exercise judgement and restraint in carrying out a particular activity

With this equation in mind, I will then seek to explain how the different variables interact to allow one to estimate the severity of an Addiction when it's present. The application of this equation will then be illustrated with some examples.

Of course, this concept is purely hypothetical in nature, but it does allow a simple way of conceptualizing the scale of any addiction, which is a disorder of varying psychosocial dimensions and magnitude.

The variables in this equation are dependent on the ***response of the individual to the addictive substance or behaviour***. This is important as different individuals react differently to different substances or behaviours and it is more important to measure their responses rather than the intrinsic properties of the substance or behaviour, which may affect individuals differently. An example being for gaming where different individuals get attracted to different types of games and some games may not evoke a pleasurable response in some people. Hence the addictiveness of a game is a measure then of how it changes or affects the variables mentioned above for the individuals concerned, rather than just on the intrinsic properties of the game itself.

In the above equation, we state that the severity of an Addiction is equal to the addition of Pleasure and Urge multiplied by Speed Squared, divided by Control. Notice that Speed is Squared, highlighting the importance of Speed in this equation.

Let us take the case of someone who is shooting up Heroin for instance and has been diagnosed with an Opioid dependence. He is shooting up Heroin many times a day and he has a seeming inability to stop or reduce his use. He describes a desire to stop using Heroin but reports strong withdrawal symptoms as well when he stops using. As a result, he is unable to reduce or stop his usage. Otherwise, he does not derive much pleasure from using Heroin.

Usually at the initial phases of a substance use disorder, the pleasure derived from using a drug is high and the urge for using is low. The urge to use a drug has often been described as cravings. As an addiction progresses, the pleasure derived from using substances gradually diminishes and instead the withdrawal symptoms set in and the urge for using the drug to alleviate distress and withdrawal symptoms then becomes paramount. It is often at the latter stage when the distressing symptoms set in that the person would either seek treatment for it or relapse back to drug use to alleviate the symptoms.

Therefore, usually as the addiction progresses, the pleasure from drug use drops and the "urge" to use the drugs to maintain some semblance of being able to cope with the withdrawal symptoms increases. For this reason, pleasure and urge are put in a bracket together in the equation as they are intricately linked with each other (Figure 1).

As can be seen in Figure 1, the intensity of liking (pleasure obtained) goes down over time whereas the intensity of cravings (urges) goes up over time as the addiction progresses. Initially the user takes drugs rather impulsively for the pleasurable sensations (the impulsive user) but thereafter as the addiction progress, does so compulsively, in the sense that he or she no longer obtains much pleasure from drug use but is unable to resist using drugs, due to the need to relieve negative sensations or withdrawal symptoms that would otherwise set in (the compulsive user).

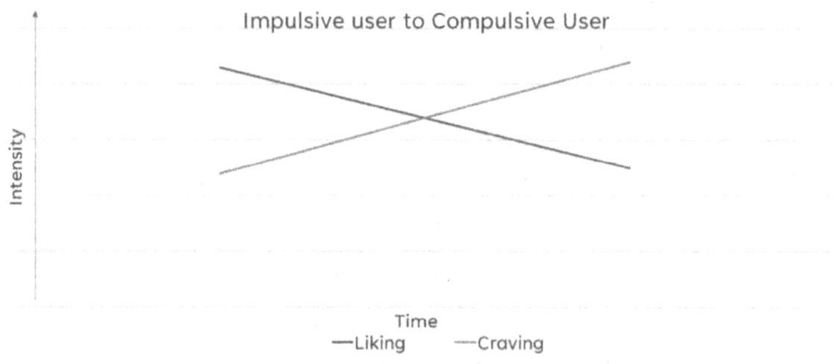

Figure 1.   Physiological and psychological changes over time.

As an addiction progresses, the control over drug use also decreases, making the denominator smaller over time, with a resultant increase in the severity of the addiction.

Notice that we have not really talked about speed yet for this equation based on the above example. The frequency that the user shoots up Heroin would also add to the severity of the addiction, with a higher speed of shooting up resulting in a higher severity of addiction.

This seemingly simplistic equation reflects a lot of diverse neurobiological process that are happening in the brain. It involves different neuronal circuits making up the reward pathway that forms the basis for any type of addictive disorder. The utility of this equation lies in elucidating what we can do to manage an addiction in terms of addressing the different variables and points us to potential new ways of looking at the complex problem of addictions.

Let us use another example to see how this equation works. Suppose a person spends time on the social media platform tik tok quite aimlessly, essentially "doom-scrolling" without any specific intent. He does so repetitively every day after school upon reaching home for several hours in a row. He seems to be able to stop when he wants to and take a break during mealtimes or gatherings with friends and family.

In this case, the urge to surf social media is quite low and he is essentially scrolling to see whether any video catches his eye. There is an instant gratification when he sees an interesting video and a pleasant sensation is felt albeit temporarily. In this case, pleasure + urge is not high as the urge to scroll is low and the pleasant sensations that are derived from "doom-scrolling" are also not high. However, the speed at which this instant gratification occurs can be very fast as the feeds on social media tend to happen rapidly, making the (pleasure + urge) × Speed^2 high in this regard. What's important is that speed is squared in this equation, highlighting its importance. In terms of control, there is still somewhat good control at using social media as he can stop as and when necessary for meals or gatherings.

Let's take this equation a step further. Is it possible to quantify the severity of addiction in terms of a numerical number for the above examples?

Suppose we use the following scales:
Pleasure: 1–5, where 1 is almost no pleasure, 2 is little pleasure, 3 is moderate pleasure, 4 is significantly high pleasure and 5 is very high pleasure, measured in terms of the degree or magnitude of positive sensations derived from an activity.

Urge: 1–5, where 1 is almost no urge, 2 is little urge, 3 is moderate degree of urge, 4 is significant urge and 5 is very high degree of urge, measured in terms of the desire to use a substance or perform a particular activity.

Speed: 1–5, where 1 is activity that takes place very slowly, 2 where activity is slow, 3 where activity is moderate in speed, 4 where activity is fast and 5 where the activity takes place very rapidly.

Control: 1–5, where 1 is almost no control, 2 is little control, 3 is moderate degree of control, 4 is a lot of control and 5 is absolute control over a particular activity.

In terms of the equation, the maximum score that can be derived is

$$(5 + 5) \times 5^2 / 1 = 250$$

The minimum score that can be derived is

$$(1 + 1) \times 1^2/5 = 2/5$$

So, the range is from 2/5 to 250, when we quantify the severity of an addiction using the above equation.

Let's use the first example again of the person who is shooting up Heroin. He is shooting up Heroin many times a day and he has a seeming inability to stop or reduce his use. He describes a desire to stop using Heroin and reports strong withdrawal symptoms as well when he stops using, hence he is unable to reduce or stop his usage. Otherwise, he does not derive much pleasure from using Heroin.

$$\text{Severity of addiction} = (2 + 5) \times 4^2/1 = 112$$

For the first example, I have indicated pleasure as 2, urge as 5, speed as 4 and control as 1. The reason being, as mentioned in the scenario, the person does not really derive much pleasure from shooting up Heroin but is unable to stop shooting up due to the presence of withdrawal symptoms when he tries to. Hence the urge is high as there is a need to continue shooting up to prevent undesired consequences. The speed is high as he is shooting up many times a day. I have indicated this as 4 in this case as there have been some instances where the use is almost throughout the day and that would be indicated as 5. Also, I have indicated that control is 1, as there is a seeming inability to control his using of Heroin.

Of course, this is just my way of conceptualizing the above scenario and different people may score the variables differently as this is highly dependent on the specifics of the actual case assessment.

Let's look at the second example. A person scrolls social media on tik tok quite aimlessly, essentially "doom-scrolling" without any functional purpose. He does so repetitively every day after school upon reaching home for several hours in a row. He seems to be able to stop when he wants to and take a break during mealtimes with family. However, in other instances, for example, he would prioritize

this activity over going out with his friends or family outdoors. In this case, the urge to surf social media is quite low and he is essentially scrolling to see whether any video catches his eye and to pass time. There is an instant gratification when he sees an interesting video and a pleasant sensation is felt.

$$\text{Severity of addiction} = (2 + 1) \times 5^2/3 = 25$$

In this case, the pleasure derived from social media surfing is labelled as a 2 as there is some degree of pleasure obtained or instant gratification from the activity. I have classified urge as 1 as the person himself has identified that there are no real cravings for him or her to use social media. The speed of use is tremendous as he or she could potentially be surfing many feeds in a hour, sometimes hundreds if not thousands, hence this variable is given a 5 here. As for control, as there is somewhat control over using, with him being able to stop the activity for important events such as for mealtimes with family but not for other activities when he is required to go outdoors. This variable is hence being given a rating of 3.

The total score for the first example is 112 whilst the score for the second example is 25.

I would consider that the first example represents a high severity of addiction whilst the second one represents a low severity.

What are the ranges for low, moderate and high severity?

Is a score of 100 high? Is a score of 10 low?

I would define the range of 2/5 to 25 as an addiction of low severity, 26 to 100 as moderate severity and 101 to 250 as high in severity. The higher the number, the greater the severity of the addiction, like a continuous variable. So, the banding is just a simple way of remembering and is really arbitrary.

First and foremost, to emphasize again, the utility of this equation is not in diagnosing if someone has an addiction. It is to determine the severity of an addiction, after someone has been diagnosed as suffering from one.

Secondly, this equation helps in the sequential monitoring of a person's addiction over time, to provide a systematic measure of sorts, to determine if his addiction is improving, worsening, or staying the same.

Lastly, this equation helps in defining the areas that therapists, psychiatrists, addiction counsellors etc can provide interventions in, to ameliorate a person's addiction. The details of such therapy will be covered in chapter 7.

The variables in this equation are pleasure, urge, speed and control. To effectively manage an addiction, one needs to decrease the pleasure, urge and speed and increase the amount of control. In order to provide meaningful interventions, it's perhaps important to explain a little about the neurobiological underpinnings behind these variables.

Pleasure is a measure of the positive sensations or positive feedback derived from a rewarding stimulus, i.e. the magnitude of such positive feedback. These are primal drives and usually the nidus of such primal drives lies in our limbic system. Similarly, urge is a function of processes lodged in the limbic system, these processes of withdrawal and tolerance and the need to mediate such negative affective symptoms usually reside in structures such as the amydala, hippocampus and the circuits are usually found in the mesolimbic pathways. More will be covered on this later.

Conversely, speed and control are more to do with the motor system and executive functioning. The locus of such activities lies in the pre-frontal cortex. The pre-frontal cortex is the most highly evolved area of the brain responsible for motor control, judgement, and executive functioning. This area of the brain determines how fast or slow we perform actions, how much control we exert over our day-to-day activities and essentially forms the basis of our higher cortical functions.

Simply put, what medications, therapy or counselling are trying to achieve to help someone with an addiction, is to try to reduce the pleasure, urges and the speed in executing an addiction whilst increasing the amount of control someone has.

In order to do this, treatment has to be targeted towards improving the functioning of the pre-frontal circuit to enable a person to increase his or her control over the addiction and to reduce the speed of doing a particular behaviour. Treatment can also be directed at reducing the pleasure or euphoric sensations derived from or reducing the urges or cravings for the addictive behaviours. This can be achieved through medications or therapy that aim to reduce the association of pleasurable sensations with particular activities or increasing aversion associated with particular activities to make them less rewarding or stimulating. Therapy or medications can also help in reducing the biological impulses or cravings to use drugs or perform certain addictive behaviours.

Indeed, how to do so is then subject to the chemical properties of the medication and or particular modality used in therapy. For instance, cognitive behavioural therapy to help patients identify the triggers for particular behaviours and then practising homework to enable greater mastery of a person's internal reactions to such triggers can help in a person attaining greater control over his or her actions. This will help in reducing the severity of an addiction. Similarly, mindfulness can help in a person slowing down his or her own biorhythms and aid in **control** over a person's natural impulses and hence also reducing the severity of an addiction.

Some medications work by reducing the cravings for particular drugs, alcohol or certain behavioural addictions like gambling. Other medications reduce the pleasure derived from taking particular substances. There are also some medications that help in reducing withdrawal symptoms associated with taking certain drugs or alcohol, thereby reducing the urges to resume taking drugs or alcohol. Often times, different

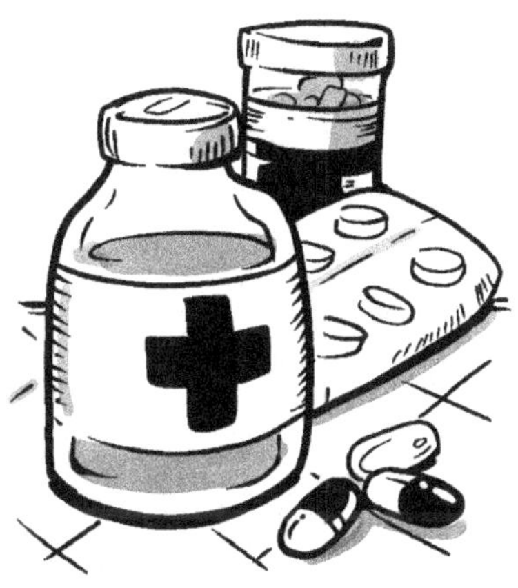

medications are used in different phases of a patient's journey with a treatment provider. For instance, medications may be used in the acute detoxification process to alleviate withdrawal symptoms and later on, medications which reduce pleasurable sensations and cravings may be used during the rehabilitation phase to maintain abstinence from the substance or behaviour.

Indeed, there are many different ways of helping someone manage an addiction. Psychosocial measures that increase the connectedness of someone to his or her own familial unit or community resources including self-help groups such as narcotics anonymous or alcoholic anonymous can also help in reducing the urge for someone using drugs and or increase the control someone has over an addictive behaviour.

The beauty of this equation is that it will help in assessing whether a particular therapy or medication is likely to be helpful if it targets these variables that help to encompass any form of addiction. Over time, charting the severity of an addiction through the result derived from this equation will help in assessing whether a patient is improving and what areas the person still needs focus on in terms of his or her treatment. More will be covered on treatments in a separate chapter.

Let's encapsulate this equation further with an example of a patient that I typically see in clinic and use it to calculate the severity of the addiction. James is a 60-year-old Chinese male who has been in and out of the drug rehabilitation centre for the past 20 years for Heroin Use. He was just released from the drug rehabilitation centre (DRC) 4 months ago for Heroin use and has relapsed to Heroin use for the past one week.

He mentioned that he was facing extreme financial distress after being released from DRC and met up with some of his old pals who were still using Heroin. They offered him some and he immediately started smoking Heroin again. He used to inject Heroin intravenously, even using his "highway" (femoral artery) to inject on occasion but has not done so yet after being released from the drug rehabilitation centre. He experiences intense pleasure after smoking Heroin and said he felt "refreshed" having not used it for close to 2 years. He has some cravings for Heroin and his use quickly escalated for the past one week, currently smoking up to 2 straws of Heroin in one day, spreading his use over the day, several puffs every few hours.

He is worried that his use will escalate further to intravenous use and he is worried about going back to the drug rehabilitation centre. He mentions that now he will experience mild withdrawal symptoms and cravings now when he does not use Heroin for more than half a day and is looking for an admission to detoxify himself from Heroin, saying that he is unable to control his use outside if he is not admitted. His last use of Heroin was 6 hours prior to seeing you and he is already feeling moderate cravings for Heroin now. He feels that his control for Heroin use is not much and is worried that he will relapse to using Heroin soon.

Based on the above scenario, what is the severity of James' Heroin use?

Let's revise again what is the addiction equation?

$$\text{Severity of Addiction} = \frac{(\text{Pleasure} + \text{Urge}) \times \text{Speed}^2}{\text{Control}}$$

Pleasure: 1–5, where 1 is almost no pleasure, 2 is little pleasure, 3 is moderate pleasure, 4 is significantly high pleasure and 5 is very high pleasure, measured in terms of the degree or magnitude of positive sensations derived from an activity.

Urge: 1–5, where 1 is almost no urge, 2 is little urge, 3 is moderate degree of urge, 4 is significant urge and 5 is very high degree of urge, measured in terms of the desire to use a substance or perform a particular activity.

Speed: 1–5, where 1 is activity that takes place very slowly, 2 where activity is slow, 3 where activity is moderate in speed, 4 where activity is fast and 5 where the activity takes place very rapidly.

Control: 1–5, where 1 is almost no control, 2 is little control, 3 is moderate degree of control, 4 is a lot of control and 5 is absolute control over a particular activity.

For this scenario, I would quantify pleasure as 5 as James has just restarted his use of Heroin and describes the feeling of pleasure as intense, which signifies very high degree of pleasure from using. In terms of urge, James described some cravings for using Heroin, but is able to spread his use of Heroin every few hours, smoking 2 straws of Heroin a day. I would quantify his urge as mild in nature as he reports only mild cravings and withdrawal symptoms when not using, Hence his urge can be quantified as 2. In terms of speed of use, his use of Heroin is every few hours, taking a few puffs each time. In terms of Heroin use, this speed is considered slow and can be quantified as 2. In terms of control, he described little control over his Heroin use and felt that he would relapse to Heroin soon without an admission. Hence his control can be quantified as 2 as well.

Hence, severity of James' Heroin addiction is as follows.

$$\text{Addiction severity} = (5 + 2) \times 2^2/2 = 7 \times 4/2 = 14$$

Based on the following reference points
2/5–25: low severity
26–100: moderate severity
101–250: high severity

James' addiction severity is thus low in nature. Hopefully with this case description, it has helped us anchor how to quantify the severity of addiction using the addiction equation. We can also use this equation to track James' progress over time.

QUIZ TIME 1:

1. Which area of the brain is responsible for decision making, executive functioning and helps inhibit addictive impulses?

   a) Frontal Lobe

   b) Occipital Lobe

   c) Temporal Lobe

   d) Parietal Lobe

2. Where are the centres of the brain responsible for the generation of pleasurable sensations?

   a) Pituitary gland

   b) Occipital Lobe

   c) Limbic system

   d) Parietal Cortex

3. As an addiction progresses over time, generally which of the following is true?

    a) Pleasure decreases and cravings decreases

    b) Pleasure decreases and cravings increases

    c) Pleasure increases and cravings increases

    d) Pleasure increases and cravings decreases

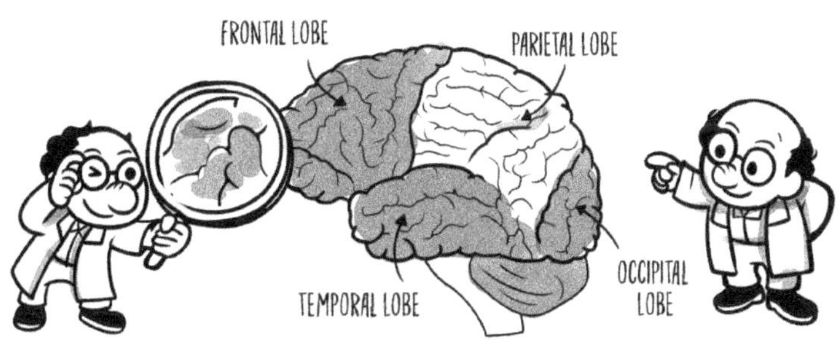

2

DO I HAVE AN ADDICTION?

I often had friends ask me if they suffer from an addiction. Some have asked me if they have a shopping addiction, others have asked me if they have an eating addiction. Whilst there are some addictions that have already been identified and validated in the literature, other types of addiction have only little supporting evidence and still others are more pop culture than real addictions.

Take for example my friend, whom I shall refer to as Miss S. Miss S spends 10k a month shopping online for stuff, something she calls retail therapy. She buys an assortment of things, from shoes, cosmetics, wines to handbags and jewellery. Usually, she pays the credit card bills herself and doesn't accrue any debts. However, recently she has forgotten to pay some of these bills due to her busy work as a marketing professional. As a result, she has incurred late interest payments on some of these bills and her family is getting concerned about her spending. Miss S herself says she shops to alleviate the stress from her stressful job of working long hours and having to find clients to sustain the company. She says that shopping online and buying things makes her feel better about her situation and helps her cope.

She mentions that she has only forgotten to pay her bills once or twice, not because of a lack of money but really because she has genuinely forgotten to do so due to her busy schedule. She says that spending 10K a month on shopping is definitely feasible due to her income and she says her family members are just being overly concerned. She acknowledges that she is still otherwise functioning well in her work and that she is still having an active social lifestyle mingling with friends and having good relationships with her family, despite the recent kerfuffle over the late payment of credit card bills. Does Miss S have a shopping addiction? What do you think?

How do we determine if a person is suffering an addiction? Currently the standard of diagnosis lies in the diagnostic and statistical manual volume 5, otherwise known as DSM-5 or the international classification of diseases volume 11, otherwise known as ICD-11. These diagnostic manuals specify certain criteria for different types of addictions. These features are typically seen in people with addictive disorders and once the person fulfils a certain number of criteria, then a diagnosis of an addiction can be made. The more criteria is satisfied, the more severe the addiction. Below, we explore some of the more common features seen in patients with addictive disorders. The criteria also enable clinicians to specify if patients are in early remission or sustained remission from an addiction.

One of the reasons why I have come up with the Addiction equation is that even though DSM-5 has defined severity by the number of the criteria that have been met by a person who has an addiction, very often this doesn't make much sense to me. For instance, if a person has an Alcohol Use Disorder and initially fulfilled 6 criteria (including tolerance) and is therefore classified as having a severe Alcohol Use Disorder but thereafter for instance his tolerance to alcohol has dropped tremendously due to liver failure, he now only has 5 criteria met even though he still continues to have severe cravings for alcohol and much psychosocial impairment secondary to alcohol use. Does that mean that then his condition is now moderate in severity as he now only fulfils 5 criteria? Inherently this does not make sense as his condition or his addiction is still quite severe and has not changed.

Or for that matter, if two people both fulfil 6 criteria (including cravings) for an Alcohol Use Disorder but one person drinks markedly in excess of the other and has such severe cravings that he is unable to go for more than an hour without alcohol whereas on the other hand, another person also has cravings but is able to drink only after work, satisfying his cravings only when he has finished work. In terms of DSM-5, both have a severe Alcohol Use Disorder but the first person would most definitely have a much more severe disorder. How useful then is the number of DSM-5 criteria in terms of quantifying the severity of an addiction? Inherently, the problem with DSM-5 in quantifying the severity of an addiction is that there is no weightage being given to each criterion and you would tick it off as present as long as subjectively it can be said to be fulfilled.

Also, the problem with the DSM-5 criteria is that it is not fluid or dynamic enough as we know addiction severity can change quite fast as the person moves through the stages of change (more will be covered later on this). So whilst a person may persist to have 6 criteria for instance over time, each criteria may have increased or lessened in intensity, hence making the addiction more or less severe.

Despite the shortfalls of quantifying severity based on DSM-5, it is still a much-referenced diagnostic criteria and there is much evidence behind its use, hence my critique is just my opinion and I proffer **_the addiction equation_** to help provide more insights.

Next, I discuss some of the key features that define any type of Addictions.

Salience

The hallmark feature of any addiction is the Salience of this behaviour in a person's life. Salience is the prominence of such behaviour, an overwhelming presence of such a behaviour in a person's life. If a person is suffering from an alcohol addiction, for example, then the presence of drinking should be highly prominent around this person's life, and oftentimes his or her life would revolve around alcohol.

Another example of salience is as described below in a patient who has seen me for compulsive sexual behavioural disorder. This patient reports masturbating in the toilets even whilst at work and has surfed for pornography on his work computers even though he acknowledges the risk of being discovered by his colleagues. At other times when he is out of the house and not working, he feels a constant urge to masturbate and has even masturbated at public toilets. This patient is constantly preoccupied by sexual thoughts and is unable to focus on anything else without giving in to urges and it has become intrusive into his life. Such is the meaning of salience, a preponderance of that behaviour within a person's lifestyle such that it takes front and centre stage. As a result of this salience of behaviour, the person is unable to attend to much else in his life, whether it's his family commitments or his work or other social engagements.

Control

Another hallmark feature of addictions is the loss of control. The person reports difficulty cutting down or stopping the use of substances or alcohol or in his or her engagement with certain behaviours such as gambling. There is often an inherent awareness in that individual that he or she needs to stop or cut back on his excessive drinking for instance, but the individual feels helpless to do so. Even when the person has successfully stopped the behaviour, he or she has experienced repeated episodes of slipping back to the same habits (rapid reinstatement).

Some of the patients who have seen me for alcohol use disorder often tell me that they set limits for themselves when they drink as they know that when they drink past a certain amount, the disinhibition takes over and they are no longer able to stop themselves from drinking. Similarly, patients who have seen me for gambling disorder, sometimes limit the amount of money they carry to the casinos to stop gambling after they have lost that predetermined amount, as the gambling can quickly spiral out of control if they do not have stop loss measures.

Indeed, the illusion of control is often what sufferers from an addiction think they have that often leads to a slippery slope back into a full-blown relapse. It often starts from a self-reassuring statement for example, "One or two drinks is not going to hurt" and then before you know it, the person is drinking way over what he or she intended to and then becomes intoxicated. Such is the nature of an addiction that the first of the 12 steps in Narcotics anonymous or Alcoholics Anonymous is this acknowledgement of this lack of control. It says "We admitted we were powerless over our addiction, that our lives had become unmanageable".

One of the patients that I had seen before, whom I shall refer to as Mr. X, has had a problem concerning alcohol and has been diagnosed with a severe alcohol use disorder. He has ended up in hospital multiple times after being intoxicated to the extent that sometimes, he will even end up with severe complications due to his drinking such as developing delirium tremens, which is a state of altered consciousness and disturbed bodily functions with a high mortality or death rate if left untreated. The reason why he frequently ends up in this state is due partly to this illusion of control which he believes he has over his drinking despite the numerous contradictory evidence based on his presentations to the emergency rooms and the hospitals. When I see him in the clinic, he will frequently tell me that he has cut down on his drinking and he is very much better compared with before, based on his levels of drinking. He then tells me what his self-imposed limit of drinking is now before saying that he has not gotten intoxicated in a long time.

For Mr. X, my advice to him and the goal of treatment has always been to work towards total abstinence from drinking. This is because in a patient with severe alcohol use disorder which is what Mr. X is suffering from, there is often little to no control over the drinking and any sense of control is fleeting and at best a temporary phenomenon which easily goes away after some alcohol has entered the system. Indeed, it is this illusory nature of the control that has led to slippery slopes of relapse time and time again that has resulted in his frequent hospitalizations.

Having insight of this lack of control over the drinking can make a big difference in treatment outcomes for many of my patients and the patients who have demonstrated insight into their lack of control, frequently end up doing better in treatment as compared to the patients who have this false assurance over their degree of control over their addiction.

Impairment of Function

For any person to be considered as suffering from an addictive disorder, that condition must necessarily cause an impairment to the function of that individual. That means that the disorder has negatively impacted on the functioning of that person in carrying out his or her duties at work or impacted upon his social or familial commitments. Some of my patients who have struggled with addictions have constantly missed work, not been present during family gatherings or just isolated themselves away from friends and colleagues. They usually spend a large part of their time focussed

on their addiction and this then takes them away from their day-to-day commitments. Such is the stranglehold that an addiction can have on a person's life, and it is the salience of behaviour with its accompanying negative consequences that often results in much friction within the family and that leads to chasms between the sufferer and of society at large.

This impairment of function may not be all that easy to detect, especially in a pre-morbidly highly functioning individual who has developed compensatory mechanisms to hide the impairment. Indeed, you may have heard of the term "functioning alcoholic" for instance to describe a person who is dependent on alcohol but is otherwise able to cope seemingly well with the demands of life. In such instances, the nature of the addiction would mean that these individuals are drinking alcohol more than the recommended guidelines and have other associated symptoms of addiction, possibly drinking more during stressful periods or using alcohol to cope with negative emotions. Indeed, such individuals would frequently be in denial of their addiction or even be oblivious to the harms that alcohol is causing to them (e.g. being irritable or restless when not drinking). It takes a keen eye from family members or friends to have an index of suspicion for these otherwise highly functioning individuals.

Take for example, a patient, Miss Y, who was a very highly functioning executive that has seen me for a couple of years. Initially, prior to seeing me, she was at the top of her field, always getting the coveted contracts that she negotiated for and raking in big investments for her company. Insidiously, however, she started drinking more during her social functions with her clients and found that it took the edge off her work. Over time, she was getting more and more hangovers and even developed blackouts on occasions. Thereafter with more and more blackouts, she noticed her memory deteriorating. Soon after, her functioning and performance at work also deteriorated even though she was still considered performing way ahead of her peers. The only obvious telling sign of her addiction was that she was no longer attending as many cell group sessions as before and her cell group members started raising this concern to her husband who then started noticing the appearance of more and more bottles of wine at home and became suspicious of her drinking.

Upon further observation, her husband noticed that she was also reporting for work later and claiming to be working from home even though she was really nursing bad hangovers.

At this instance, then he decided to bring her to seek treatment.

What this case scenario then highlights is that sometimes, this impairment of function is not that obvious as Miss Y was still performing well at work and somewhat socially as her husband was not aware of her heavy drinking till her close friends at church noticed her absence. This was when he started to pay more attention to her and noticed the problems related to her drinking.

Not all Present the Same Way

Other features of Addiction as specified in the DSM-5 include cravings, building up of tolerance, withdrawal symptoms etc. Some features are more common than others whilst some symptoms such as tolerance may not be seen for all classes of substances. A common example of this is with inhalants where the user may not necessarily develop physical dependence features of tolerance and withdrawal with prolonged use.

In the past cannabis users often did not experience withdrawal symptoms as well until more recently when more potent strains of Cannabis were discovered and then gradually even users of Cannabis started showing withdrawal symptoms. The important point to note here is that a person who is addicted to a substance need not exhibit all the features of an addiction. Another important point which is seldom highlighted, is that different individuals who have an addiction may exhibit different symptoms even if they are addicted to the same substance. Person A may repeatedly use alcohol in hazardous situations, e.g. whilst operating heavy machinery whilst Person B may not, and both may still be addicted to alcohol.

Similarly, Person X may report strong cravings for Methamphetamine whilst Person Y may not, and both may still be addicted to Methamphetamine.

As long as the individuals concerned have fulfilled a mandatory minimum number of criteria as specified in the DSM-5 or ICD 11, they can be diagnosed as suffering from an addiction. It is also worth noting that many individuals suffering from an addiction often do minimize the symptoms that they are experiencing when asked as it can be difficult for one to acknowledge that he or she is having an addiction or be seen as impaired from this illness. This is the stigma of suffering from an addiction, and we should therefore be sensitive when asking questions pertaining to these symptoms.

Behavioural Addictions

There are only a few behavioural addictions that have been identified in literature. Gambling was the very first behaviour that was demonstrated to be addictive in scientific literature and was the first to build up enough evidence base to be classified as an addiction in DSM-5. Prior to DSM-5, Gambling Disorder was classified under DSM-IV as an impulse control disorder and was given the label of Pathological Gambling. Thereafter, in ICD-11, Gaming Disorder then came onto the bandwagon as an Addictive behaviour even though DSM-5 has not officially recognized it as an addictive disorder per se, rather including the term internet gaming disorder as a condition in Section III as a condition deserving of further research.

Hence, there are differences even between different diagnostic manuals in terms of behavioural addictions that are listed. In ICD-11, there was also a new diagnosis termed

Compulsive Sexual Behavioural Disorder, which is under the category of impulse control disorders. This condition though, has had many debates as to whether it should be called an addiction instead, specifically sex addiction, since it shares many similarities with an addictive disorder.

Does this mean then that other behavioural addictions are not legitimate. Unfortunately, science does take a while to catch up whilst there are new things being developed every day. For instance, in this new age of social media and generative AI, pretty much something new in the digital realm comes about every day at breakneck speeds. We will talk about such new world online digital addictions a bit further in a separate chapter as I feel it deserves more emphasis and discussion.

Let's discuss the notion of there being other behavioural addictions. Is there such a thing as shopping addiction or food addiction? What about an exercise addiction? Are these addictions truly existent or are they more of a fad? Increasingly, new addictions are being coined, for instance social media addiction etc and we need to be mindful of whether these are truly addictions as calling anything an addiction implies that it is a disease that can and should be treated.

My opinion is that so long as you can derive pleasure from an activity, then any sort of activity can **potentially** become addictive. Some people develop what we call a runner's high after running and then continuously seek to regain some pleasurable sensations after running. Who is to say that over time, this behaviour doesn't become self-reinforcing and addictive? However, as mentioned in the principles stated above on addiction, for a behaviour to be classified as a disorder, it must cause an impairment to the functioning of the individual.

So, if a person exercising excessively does it to the point of omission of certain essential activities, causing impairment to his or her social life, then that can be considered as an addiction.

Hence, it is not so easy to be "labelled" as having an addiction as impairment of function doesn't happen to some of my friends who have asked me if they have an exercise addiction or even a shopping addiction for that matter. This diagnosis could be justified however, if they had suffered negative consequences in their relationship or in their social or occupational functioning because of the particular behaviour and for that matter if there are other associated features such as Salience or impairment of control that was discussed earlier.

Uncommon Addictions

Over the course of my practice as a psychiatrist, I have seen patients seemingly getting addicted to drugs that were not really considered to be addictive. For example, there were patients who had frequently asked for the medication benzhexol, otherwise known as Artane, an anticholinergic medication. Such medications are commonly prescribed to counter extrapyramidal side effects (EPSE) from first generation anti-psychotics and some patients despite coming off first generation antipsychotics, continued to request for Artane, despite not having EPSE. There are probably complex reasons behind this, from developing a psychological dependence to Artane to Artane causing an initial euphoric reaction for some people. Whatever the reason may be, the truth is, any drug can potentially be addictive if a person can derive some pleasurable benefits from it. Indeed, it has been quite trying to de-prescribe Artane for some of these patients and whilst there may not be much physical symptoms coming off Artane, the psychological attachment and problems coping without the medication are very real.

Another well-known example is pregabalin. This is an anti-seizure medication that is also used to treat pain and has indications for anxiety as well. I have observed patients who are on this medication for anxiety to have escalating use of it due to a build-up of tolerance and patients have become addicted to it as well. Another similar example is Gabapentin, with similar indications for use. There are certain medications which have a propensity for patients to become dependent on them and we need to be mindful that these may not be limited to the sedative hypnotics like benzodiazepines and Z-drugs.

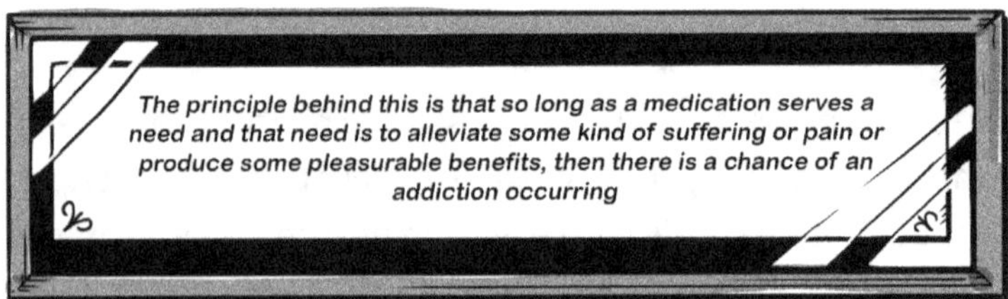

Indeed, I have treated many patients with addiction who have also come to know of this medication Pregabalin and have requested for it as it has helped to relieve their anxiety symptoms and provides sedation at night when they need it the most. It then becomes very difficult for the clinician to de-prescribe such medications and indeed some do become dependent or "addicted" to them with chronic use.

Maintaining Internal Homeostasis

Indeed, what I like to describe to some of my patients and indeed the students that I have taught is that patients who are addicted to substances or types of additive behaviour have an imbalance of their internal neurochemistry. In order to achieve some semblance of internal homeostasis in their neurochemistry, they turn to the addiction. This state of homeostasis can be achieved when they use the substances or when we prescribe them various psychotropics. The better our medications help them achieve this internal homeostasis, the less likely they will relapse to using the illicit substances or going back to the addictive behaviour.

It's not uncommon that many patients dabble in using multiple substances to maintain this internal homeostasis. An example being a polysubstance abuser who uses a downer (central nervous system depressant) such as Heroin and also mixes it with an upper (central nervous system stimulant) such as Methamphetamine, almost like a cocktail to ensure that his internal neurochemistry stays in some kind of balance, to avoid it being too overstimulated or too depressed. Another example of patients I have seen are those with bipolar disorder who have abused different types of drugs depending on which phase of illness they are in, for example using stimulants when they are in the depressed phase and using central nervous system depressants such as benzodiazepines or alcohol when they are in the manic phase. Again, these are based on my observations and the likely scenario is that these patients are being their own doctors and trying to maintain some semblance of internal homeostasis.

In the literature, what has been found is that certain types of antidepressants have been found to be helpful for patients who abuse psychostimulants such as methamphetamine. These include antidepressants such as mirtazapine and bupropion and a hypothesis then is that these patients who are abusing psychostimulants are perhaps prone to depression and are hence using psychostimulants as a form of self-medication or prophylactic measure.

Indeed, internal balance is essential for all of us to function and perhaps having an internal neurochemical thermostat that is faulty due to the hijacking of this reward pathway is something that patients with addiction constantly suffer from, leading to a state of imbalance.

Differential Diagnosis

When you see a friend or family member seemingly doing something repetitively, it's important to find out the underlying reason. Not all people who repetitively do something to the exclusion of everything else are suffering from an addiction. There are important differential disorders to consider. For instance, obsessive compulsive disorder (OCD) or possibly even an eating disorder. Let me explain further below.

Individuals with OCD suffer from obsessions and compulsions. For instance, an individual with OCD may keep having certain thoughts, for instance repetitive thoughts pertaining to whether they have done something correctly or whether their hands are clean, and they may perform certain rituals, for example checking rituals or hand washing rituals to ensure that they have done certain things correctly or that their hands are clean. These actions help to relieve the anxiety that stem from the thoughts. It may appear that they cannot control their actions, like individuals with addictions who compulsively use drugs or who gamble.

However, the difference is that such individuals with OCD experience distress when performing such rituals and their actions are ego-dystonic (in opposition to the will). These means that individuals with OCD do not want to do these actions in the first place. This is as opposed to consuming drugs or alcohol where the action itself of consuming drugs or alcohol was initially as a means to derive pleasure and is ego-syntonic (in accordance with the will). Thereafter however, once an addiction is formed, the compulsiveness of the behaviour then takes over. The individual may no longer experience pleasurable sensations from taking drugs or alcohol but continues to do so to relieve the negative sensations of withdrawal that would otherwise ensue.

Having an eating disorder, for instance binge eating disorder, is another such condition that could potentially be confused for an addiction. Such individuals with binge-eating disorder are often obese and have difficulty controlling what they eat, often eating in extremes. However, this is not to be confused with having an addiction to food. Currently whilst there is some evidence behind food addiction as a medical condition, there is insufficient evidence based on existing literature to classify it as a diagnosable medical disease.

In the literature, there have been different scales used to measure food addiction and the Yale Food Addiction Scale is one such tool for measuring food addiction. However, suffice to say here that certain "addictions" have not yet made it to mainstream diagnosable diseases and we should be careful in labelling people with such conditions. This applies to other pop culture addictions such as shopping addiction and exercise addiction for instance.

I understand that this contrasts with what I have said earlier about anything in the world possibly being addictive when someone is able to derive pleasure from it. However, even though some of these conditions do not yet surface in the realm of addictions as defined by DSM or ICD, this is not to say that some people do not genuinely suffer from distressing symptoms from these conditions. For instance, I have had colleagues who are genuinely distressed by how much money they spend on retail therapy in a month and have raked up huge credit card debts from it. Do some of these people have an impulse control issue- for sure. However, there is currently insufficient evidence to classify these conditions as addictions and at best we can try to use similar principles to help some of these individuals suffering from such impulse control issues using cognitive behavioural techniques as will be discussed later.

Evolving Field of Behavioural Addictions

Some of the patients I have seen have self-referred for sex-addiction. Currently, there is a condition called compulsive sexual behavioural disorder (CSBD) which is an impulse control disorder recently added to ICD-11 (International classification of diseases, version 11). Whilst not listed as an addictive behaviour in ICD-11, it has features similar to an addiction such as the failure or loss of control. It remains to be seen if CSBD would eventually be relabelled as a behavioural addiction with further research. This happened for Gambling, which went from Pathological Gambling, an impulse Control Disorder in DSM-IV to Gambling Disorder, an addiction in DSM-5, so I believe the jury is still out there for CSBD as well. So despite the term sex addiction commonly being bandied about, there is still no official diagnosis, at least based on DSM-5 or ICD-11 and the term is used loosely even though CSBD does closely resemble it.

Gaming Disorder on the other hand has been listed in ICD-11 as a behavioural addiction. What does this imply for the field of behavioural addictions? I believe this field is still in its nascent stages of growth and is by no means already complete. There is still much to explore about behavioural addictions and perhaps we will get new diagnoses as more research evidence comes up.

Blurring of Diagnostic Boundaries

The field of addictions has an overlap with other fields and share certain elements such as compulsiveness of behaviours, so it is often not so easy to distinguish from some of the other disorders mentioned earlier. People who have self-referred for sex-addiction can for instance be diagnosed with paraphilic disorders instead. I have seen individuals who report a compulsive need to cross dress to sexually stimulate themselves. They present to my clinic thinking that they have a sex-addiction whereas in fact they suffer from a paraphilic disorder. Other individuals display paraphilic or voyeuristic behaviour such as taking upskirt photos or spying on other people using toilets respectively and again present themselves at my clinic believing that they suffer from a sex-addiction. Indeed, some of these individuals may have a co-morbid sex addiction or compulsive sexual behavioural disorder but more often than not, they suffer from a paraphilic disorder instead which is a form of sexual deviancy rather than a sex addiction.

To illustrate how fast the field of behavioural addictions is growing, I have devoted an entire chapter on new world addictions which has been termed "digital Heroin" by psychotherapist Nicholas Kardaras. These digital addictions have the insidious propensity to take over large chunks of our time and attention, e.g. new world fads such as social media and different types of online multiplayer games that build their own worlds and narratives and which our Youth are increasingly being exposed to nowadays. The rapid development of this field is both interesting and concerning as we are constantly being inundated with new devices and online media, zapping away at our attention. These topics will be covered in chapter 5.

QUIZ TIME 2:

1. Which of the following has not been classified as an addiction in either ICD-11 or DSM 5?

   a) Gambling Disorder

   b) Gaming Disorder

   c) Sex Addiction

   d) Alcohol use Disorder

2. Which of the following is listed as a behavioural addiction in ICD-11 but not in DSM-5?

   a) Gaming Disorder

   b) Internet Gaming Disorder

   c) Gambling Disorder

   d) Compulsive Sexual Behavioural Disorder

3. Which of the following symptoms is not a core feature of an addiction?

   a) Salience

   b) Physical Dependence features: Tolerance and Withdrawal symptoms

   c) Lack of Control

   d) Paranoia

3

THEORIES BEHIND ADDICTIONS

 CHAPTER 3

In the past 2 chapters, we have discussed what is the addiction equation and we have also discussed what it means to have an addiction in terms of the symptoms one commonly sees in someone suffering from an addiction. However, what is the underlying basis for someone developing an addiction, what is the mechanism that leads to someone developing an addiction? Can it happen to everyone? Why are some people more prone to developing an addiction. We will explore some of the concepts behind addiction in this chapter. However, first let's talk about risk factors for addiction.

Risk Factors for Addiction

There are indeed many risk factors for developing an addictive illness. Some common risk factors include having a family history of addictions. Having a family history of addictions plays an important role not just in terms of having a genetic predisposition towards addictions, but also exposing a person early on in life towards drug use or other addictive behaviours. This then leads to mechanisms of conditioning and modelling which we will cover later in this chapter.

Besides having a family history of addictions, other environmental factors such as social influences, availability of substances in the environment and adverse childhood experiences can also lead to a higher risk of developing an addiction.

There are also many co-morbid mental health conditions that may lead to a higher risk of developing an addiction. For instance, having depression, anxiety, attention deficit hyperactivity disorder can also predispose someone to developing an addiction.

How do these risk factors interact to cause someone to develop an addiction and what are the models behind addiction will be covered in this chapter.

Take for example my patient Mr. JT, he is a 30-year-old man whose both parents have been incarcerated many times since he was a young boy, for drug related offences. Mr. JT was brought up by his grandparents since he was young and he would get to see his parents on and off only when they were out of prison. He grew up in an impoverished neighbourhood and got exposed to smoking early on in life. Thereafter, he and his neighbourhood friends got involved in gangs and this led to a cycle of petty thefts, fights and drug use.

Eventually by the time he was 19 years of age, he had used cannabis, cough mixture, sleeping pills and this then escalated to his eventual use of Heroin.

JT would never fit-in in school and he was used to fending for himself since young, preferring to live off the streets. Hence when he was enlisted into National Service, he had problems obeying authority and listening to commands. This led to repeated cycles of insubordination and multiple sentences to the detention barracks. Eventually he was discharged from National Service, where he continued to associate with his drug using peers.

This cycle went on and he was eventually sentenced to the drug rehabilitation centre after being arrested for Heroin use, shortly after his release from National Service. This cycle of going in and out of the drug rehabilitation centre eventually culminated into a long term sentence subsequently in prison itself and he had spent a good 15 years in and out of prison by the time he was 50 years old.

As can be seen in the above example, JT had a lot of risk factors for drug use since he was born. Both parents using drugs, living in an impoverished neighbourhood, social deprivation, early smoking etc, were all significant risk factors for him continuing to use drugs. Indeed, then drug addiction is as much a social problem as it is a medical one.

The Role of Dopamine and Other Neurotransmitters

It has often been said that dopamine is the neurotransmitter responsible for "pleasure". This rush of dopamine in our brains, in response to a stimulus that causes pleasure is what makes us feel good and in return makes us want to do more of a particular activity. However, this simple explanation is probably an oversimplification of the entire reward pathway in the brain with its numerous connections between the different anatomical structures.

Whilst dopamine is an important neurotransmitter that gives rise to the sensation of pleasure and perhaps the quintessential one, there are often many different intermediary neurotransmitters interacting with each other, affecting the production of dopamine. For example, LSD and Ecstasy work via serotonin receptors. Alcohol, Benzodiazepines and Barbiturates work via GABA receptors whilst nicotine via Acetylcholine receptors for instance. The truth is most drugs work via a combination of different neurotransmitters, producing the end-result of an increased dopaminergic surge.

The reward pathway in the brain is highly complex, having evolved from its underpinnings as a survival mechanism in our ancestors, the primordial cavemen. This pathway seeks to maximize survival above all else for the human species. So, things such as food, water, and sex etc are prioritized above other matters. This basal reward pathway is mainly seated within the limbic system of the brain, which involves the more deep-seated areas. These areas are important to ensure that our basic needs are met and are important for survival.

Gradually as the human species evolved, higher cognitive functions developed which are centred in the four cortices of the brain, with the frontal cortex in particular, being the evolved higher centre of the brain responsible for decision making, judgement and also serving as the primary motor cortex of the brain. The dorsolateral prefrontal cortex (DLPFC) in particular is often considered to be the most evolved part of the brain due to its role in reasoning, making complex decisions and modulating other aspects of behaviour.

This frontal cortex together with midbrain structures such as the ventral tegmental area, and limbic structures such as the nucleus accumbens are involved in feedback loops which regulate our reward pathway.

The limbic system, ventral tegmental area (VTA) and the frontal lobe have different feedback circuits transmitting upwards from the VTA to the limbic system and the frontal lobe and back downwards to regulate the reward circuitry of the brain. Broadly speaking, the frontal lobe exhibits inhibitory control over the ventral tegmental area and nucleus accumbens and helps to regulate the dopaminergic surges that occur in the limbic system when pleasurable sensations are experienced from various activities.

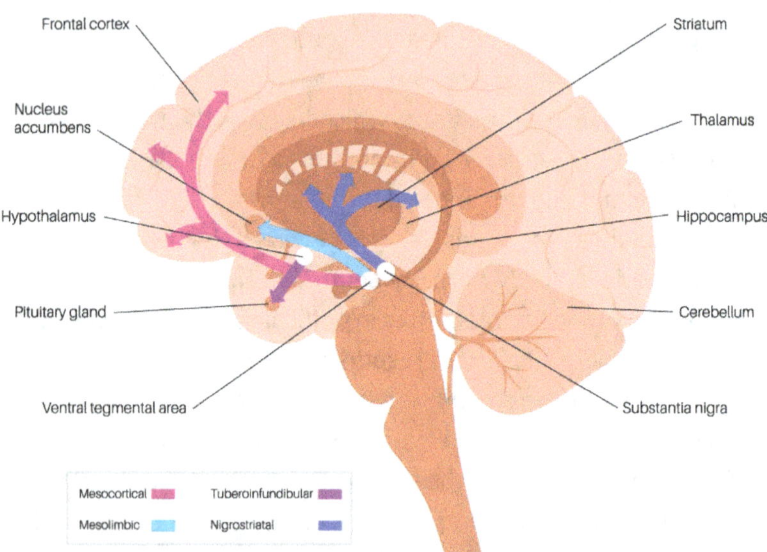

Dopamine pathway in the human brain. Monoamine neurotransmitter. Motivational component of reward motivated behavior. Motor control, controlling the release of various hormones vector illustration.
Source: https://www.shutterstock.com/image-vector/dopamine-pathway-human-brain-monoamine-neurotransmitter-2055458105

When a person uses a drug of abuse such as Heroin, over-time, this reward pathway is hijacked such that it becomes sensitized towards such drugs of abuse. The limbic system becomes "triggered" when the user is exposed to images, sounds, smells of Heroin for instance and these signals then get relayed to the subcortical structures such as the Hippocampus (which processes memories) and the amygdala (which processes emotions). When these subcortical structures get activated, the various parts of the reward pathway involving the nucleus accumbens, ventral tegmental area and the frontal cortex also get activated. During these instances, there are two competing forces. The competing desire to continue using the drug to sustain the pleasurable sensations from the constant release of dopamine originating in the sub-cortical anatomical structures versus the frontal cortex exhibiting inhibitory control over all these impulses. ***Ultimately, which decision is made is dependent on the state of the user's mind then***.

Research has shown that addiction can be divided into 3 stages, the binge/intoxication stage initially, followed by the withdrawal/negative affect stage and the preoccupation anticipation stage at the end.[1] These involve the different structures described earlier with the basal ganglia being involved mostly in the binge intoxication stage, followed by the amygdala and connecting structures in the withdrawal/negative affect stage followed by predominantly the prefrontal cortex in the last stage. Suffice for this book, that for a basic understanding of addictions, what is discussed here is adequate.

For a person who has been severely dependent on a substance with substantial cravings and a reward system that is intensely cued in on the substance of abuse, then the basal impulses of using that particular substance would trump any ability to restrict usage from the frontal lobe inhibitory control. When this patient who is severely addicted then enters treatment, what treatment does is to enable the person to gain greater confidence and ability to utilize what he has learnt through the various psychological therapies, to be able to resist the basal urges to use the drugs. Such therapies involve the use of various treatment approaches, e.g. motivational interviewing, cognitive behavioural therapies etc. which would be covered in separate sections of this book, so as to be able to strengthen the inhibitory controls exerted through the frontal cortex as well as to reduce the excitatory impulses that emerge when exposed to stimuli that trigger the urge to use a particular substance.

Besides psychological therapies that strengthen the inhibitory control, there are also pharmacological treatment options that serve to reduce the cravings or satiation derived from the substance/behaviour in the person who is addicted when exposed to the same stimuli.

In a nutshell, a person who is addicted to drugs of abuse or any other addictive behaviours has an over-excited reward pathway in the brain which can easily be hijacked when exposed to certain stimuli that triggers emotions or memories that activate the reward pathway. This pathway can become over-kindled or run autonomously if the corresponding inhibitory controls are not functioning well enough to provide the counterbalancing force.

There are many other neurotransmitters involved in addictions and dopamine is just one of them albeit a very important one that is the one responsible for the euphoric (feel good) feeling that reinforces the taking of a substance or that reinforces a particular behaviour. Neurotransmitters such as GABA, serotonin, endorphins, NMDA, acetylcholine etc all act via intermediary pathways to regulate the connections between the anatomical structures mentioned earlier which are all part of the reward pathway.

Indeed, the reward pathway can be seen to be a rather dynamic pathway with feedback loops in many directions between the different anatomical structures involved in it. This pathway reacts to the behaviours by either upregulating or downregulating its receptors in response to the release of dopamine and over time, there can even be structural changes seen in terms of the size of the anatomical structures in this reward pathway.

This doesn't mean that once the reward pathway has been hijacked and "over-kindled", it cannot be dampened. Indeed, there have been neuroimaging studies that show that some of these changes can be reversed when drug use has stopped over a period of time, accompanied by improvements in the symptoms of addiction. The same biochemical processes will take some time to re-adjust back and with prolonged abstinence, possibly even neuroanatomical changes can be seen on imaging scans of the brain.

Psychological Theories behind Addictions

Beyond the actual physiological and biological processes behind Addictions, there are also psychological theories behind Addictions as a learnt behaviour. It's important to highlight here that there are two big schools of thought behind how Addiction can develop in terms of learning theory. They are Operant Conditioning and Classical Conditioning. Let's discuss Operant Conditioning followed by Classical Conditioning.

Operant Conditioning

Operant Conditioning basically involves a system of rewards or punishments to facilitate learning. The 3 main mechanisms involved are *positive reinforcement*, *negative reinforcement* and *punishment*.

Positive reinforcement occurs when rewards are given for performing a particular behaviour. An example could be giving a star sticker to a child when he or she does his or her household chores or completes his homework. Such positive reinforcement occurs when dopamine is released in the brain after a substance of abuse is taken and causes the person to "feel-good". This principle can also be used in the treatment process of addictions to "unlearn" an addiction. An example of this is when a patient with addictions is being given vouchers to purchase daily necessities when he or she turns up for a treatment programme or abstains from drug use. This type of token economy is then used to anchor or reinforce the treatment progress made and increase the chances of a person completing a treatment regimen.

Punishment is the exact opposite of Positive reinforcement. Punishment involves delivering an aversive stimulus to a person whenever he or she performs an undesired action. An example of punishment could be a fine for instance when someone litters on the streets or is issued a corrective work order. In the context of drug use in Singapore, the most common form of punishment is perhaps a sentence to the Drug rehabilitation centre. The idea of punishment then is to deter a behaviour from taking place due to the unpleasantness from the experience of the punishment. The drug, disulfiram, for instance, given to patients with alcohol dependence, works by the principle of punishment. This drug inhibits an enzyme in the body, which then leads to the build-up of acetaldehyde when alcohol is consumed. The build-up of acetaldehyde then leads to a "flushing" reaction in the body which makes the person feel unpleasant. Hence, the person is "punished" when he or she takes alcohol after consuming disulfiram and this then works to deter the person from drinking after imbibing the medication.

Negative reinforcement on the other hand is the removal of an aversive stimulus when something desired is done by the person. For instance, when a person has chronic neck pain or back pain, sometimes manual stretching or traction when applied can help to relieve this pain. This manual stretching or traction is negative reinforcement because it takes away the pain (something negative), and therefore is reinforcing in nature. In terms of addiction, taking part in a supervised medical detoxification is negative reinforcement, because it helps to ameliorate withdrawal symptoms, making patients feel better during the detoxification process by not experiencing so much discomfort.

Next, we go on to the other aspect of learning theory, Classical Conditioning.

Classical Conditioning

Classical Conditioning is a type of associative learning in which an unconditioned stimulus that results in a response is paired repeatedly with a neutral stimulus, so as to evoke the same response when the neutral stimulus is presented alone. The neutral stimulus then becomes a conditioned stimulus.

The most classic example of this is Pavlovian conditioning in which a dog is repeatedly exposed to an unconditioned stimulus (food) that is paired repeatedly with a bell (neutral stimulus). In this case, the unconditioned stimulus of food will result in salivation when the dog is exposed to it. However, if a bell (neutral stimulus) is repeatedly rung before the food is presented, this then leads to an association of the bell ringing with food being presented and over time, just the bell ringing alone would be enough to evoke the response of salivation in the dog. This then leads to the bell becoming a conditioned stimulus.

How does this apply to drug addiction? In patients who have used drugs repeatedly, this is often associated with familiar sights and smells, that over time may trigger the urge or cravings to use drugs when the person is re-exposed to the same stimuli. Many of these external stimuli may seem innocuous to us but due to the process of conditioning in association with their past drug use habits, these neutral stimuli then become conditioned stimuli that may then trigger the urge to use drugs. An example is a person addicted to Heroin, who usually shoots up in a quiet lane in his neighbourhood for instance. One day, after being abstinent from Heroin for many months, he then passes by his old neighbourhood to buy food and passes by the familiar lane that he used to shoot up Heroin at. This passing by of a familiar lane with its familiar sights and smells then evokes old memories and triggers an urge for him to use Heroin. This is classical conditioning taking place, potentially causing the person to relapse into drug use. Therapy through CBT and mindfulness can help in dealing with the negative automatic thoughts and unhealthy behaviours that result when such conditioned stimulus is then brought up again.

There are other theories behind addictions such as social learning theory which involves interactions between the person, his or her environment as well as the addiction itself and has elements of modelling involved. Modelling essentially happens when a person role models someone else who has used drugs for instance and learns the same way of coping with adverse circumstances. Suffice to say that the different models of addiction help us conceptualize the disease better and give rise to better understanding of addiction as a multifaceted illness involving biological, psychological and social domains.

It is with this understanding that we can understand why just targeting the medical model or biological model is often not enough in addressing addictions as there are psychological and social domains which need to be managed too. For instance, even if a person has taken the medication disulfiram and is "punished" after drinking alcohol by developing a flushing reaction, it may not be enough to deter him or her from continued drinking. The person may not even use the medication in the first place if the underlying social stressors have not been resolved or if there is some psychological conflict preventing him from otherwise coping adequately.

It is with this understanding of the Biological, Psychological and Social Underpinnings of Addiction, that we can go on to the next chapter on why having an Addiction is akin to having a chronic ailment.

Reference

1. Substance Abuse and Mental Health Services Administration (US); Office of the Surgeon General (US). Facing Addiction in America: The Surgeon General's Report on Alcohol, Drugs, and Health [Internet]. Washington (DC): US Department of Health and Human Services; 2016 Nov. CHAPTER 2, THE NEUROBIOLOGY OF SUBSTANCE USE, MISUSE, AND ADDICTION.

QUIZ TIME 3:

1. Which of the following is an example of punishment?

    a) Drinking alcohol after taking disulfiram

    b) Receiving benzodiazepines to relieve withdrawal symptoms after being abstinent from alcohol

    c) Going for counselling for problems related to alcohol

    d) Receiving pain medications during the withdrawal from Heroin

2. Which are the areas of the brain most commonly involved in Addictions?

    a) VTA, Pre-frontal Cortex, Nucleus Accumbens

    b) Hypothalamus, Nucleus Accumbens, Pituitary gland

    c) Amygdala, occipital lobe, pre-frontal cortex

    d) Frontal lobe, hypothalamus and pituitary gland

3. Which of the following is not a risk factor for developing Addictions?

   a) Adverse Childhood experiences

   b) Family History of Drug use

   c) Social Deprivation

   d) Resilience

4

ADDICTION AS A CHRONIC ILLNESS

The understanding of addictions has come a long way. Initially, Addiction was thought of as a moral problem where sufferers of an addictive illness had some moral deficit or weakness in their character. During those times, people were blamed for having an addiction, for having a flaw in their character that made them use drugs and these sufferers were shunned by society. Gradually, there was more awareness of addiction as a disease. With increasing knowledge and understanding of addictions, further research was done which later led to the classification of addictions as a chronic brain disease characterized by what we mentioned in the earlier chapter in terms of imbalances in the reward pathway driven by various neurotransmitters and feedback circuits.

Recovery not Cure

Despite this understanding of addictions, treatment outcomes have not been good. The nature of addictions as chronic brain disease characterized by relapses interspersed with remissions means that we are promoting recovery from the illness rather than a cure. What is the distinction between recovery vs a cure?

When we talk about acute conditions like a cold or stomach flu, people recover fully in between episodes and hence we are cured of the cold or stomach flu. However, when we have a chronic condition like hypertension or diabetes, we are never truly cured of the condition, however the illness can be controlled with medications and a proper diet. In the same way, having an addiction is having a chronic condition whereby with proper treatment such as therapy and medications, the condition can go into remission. Similar to other chronic conditions like diabetes and hypertension, without the necessary ongoing treatment, the condition can become uncontrolled and relapse.

In addictions, remission rates are low, and the relapse rates are quite high. This is because fundamentally, the brain's wiring has changed. The responses of a person who is addicted to a particular substance or behaviour is heightened by even simple cues which may seem innocuous to a person who is not addicted. For example, when an addicted person walks past a familiar environment where he remembers a painful memory, for example a breakup with a former partner, this can trigger his hippocampus (centre for storage of memories in his brain) to fire, leading to activation of the amygdala (flight or fight response centre) and finally leading to activation of the adjacent reward pathway to soothe himself. This same pattern of firing would not be activated in a person whose reward pathway has not been changed by the addiction, when exposed to same stimulus.

So, we can understand why having an addiction is a chronic illness in the sense that whilst therapy and treatment with medications can dampen these emotional responses and over time possibly correct the way the person responds to these cues, fundamentally the person is still at risk of going back to the addiction if the circumstances are "right". That is not to say however, that with proper management of the condition, one cannot stay away from the substance or behaviour that the person is addicted to. With the right support, the aim is to prevent a relapse and enable the person to learn coping skills and build resilience to live a life away from the addiction. There is truly no panacea for this and indeed it can be a constant struggle for the person who is addicted.

Take for example my patient Mr T, a 60-year-old man who has been in and out of the drug rehabilitation centre (DRC) and prison many times, and to this day still struggles with Heroin use. He started using Heroin when he was 18 years old after being introduced to it by friends he met whilst doing part time work. After using it for about 6 months, he was heavily addicted to using Heroin, using up to one bag of Heroin a day and eventually went on to injecting Heroin. At times, he was also injecting Subutex (another opioid) to substitute for Heroin, but Heroin was the main drug he was using throughout the years.

Despite going in and out of DRC and prison, Mr. T has never been able to stop using Heroin voluntarily for prolonged periods of time after being out of the drug rehabilitation centre. Usually, he would be admitted to a halfway house for several months after his release from prison before going home to stay. However, he would relapse soon after his release from the halfway house as he always found the cravings and urges for Heroin returning when he met up with peers who were still using Heroin. The longest he has abstained from using Heroin whilst not being in a controlled environment such as a halfway house is around 10 months. Thereafter, the stress from loneliness as well as from financial stressors usually proves too overwhelming for him and he ends up using Heroin to cope.

Such is the difficulty at which my patients face when trying to cope with a drug addiction. Very often, the nature of addiction means that it is always lingering in the background, waiting for a person to be at the most vulnerable stage before staging a comeback. Hence, we celebrate milestones in a patient's recovery journey as every day that a person manages to abstain from drug use is a success in every way.

Identifying Slips or Relapses Early

One way of helping a person who is addicted is to identify a slip quickly to prevent a full-blown relapse of the condition. An example is someone who has been addicted to pornography and after a argument with his spouse, quickly turns to pornography as a coping mechanism. In this case, if he has attended enough therapy sessions to build insight and awareness into his condition and manages to identify his unhealthy coping mechanism after the initial slip back to pornography as disruptive to his recovery, then potentially he can stop the use and prevent it from spiralling into a full-blown relapse.

Indeed, studies have shown that the longer the person is abstinent from the substance or behaviour, the better he or she is able to stay in remission from the substance or behaviour addiction. Studies have also shown that the earlier the onset of an addiction, the worse the prognosis or outcome. Very often, if an addiction forms during the period of adolescence when the brain is not yet fully mature, the damage is often longer lasting. This is understandable as the neuronal circuits have not had the time to fully mature and hence the proper ways of responding to stress and adapting to maladaptive environment stimuli have not been given the time to develop. The process of neuronal "pruning" in the brain to allow the proper circuits to develop and mature in essence has been cut short by the addiction.

In Singapore, the 2022 Health and Lifestyle survey conducted by the Institute of Mental Health showed that the average age of onset of illicit drug use can be as young as 15.9 years of age, based on prevalence of drug consumption in last 12 months among Singapore residents.[1] This is quite concerning indeed as the onset of drug use could lead to the slippery slope towards development of an addiction. Currently, there have been various efforts by the central narcotics bureau (CNB) towards developing DrugfreeSG Champions who serve as agents to prevent drug use among Youth. This is an important and laudable effort as the best way to prevent a chronic disease is upstream work to prevent the onset of drug use in our Youth. It is far easier to prevent an addiction then battling an established addiction. As mentioned, earlier, once an addiction sets in, the established neuronal pathways kindle a self-perpetuating cycle and it takes much more effort to prevent a relapse.

In terms of recovery from a chronic disease, many factors play a role. This can be considered in terms of the predisposing, precipitating, perpetuating and protective factors.

Predisposing

Predisposing factors are factors that underly the onset and development of a disease. For instance, in addictions, it could be adverse childhood experiences such as being bullied, living in poverty, having family members who use drugs etc. These then present a set of conditions that make it more likely for a person to develop an addiction. Such factors are commonly a combination of both genetic and environmental influences.

Precipitating

Precipitating factors are factors that in a way trigger the onset of an addiction. These factors may overwhelm the natural coping system of an individual and hence the individual then acutely turns to drug use as a way to cope. An example of such a precipitating factor could be sudden onset of a stressful life event, e.g. a divorce, getting retrenched from a job etc. These sudden onset life events could then result in a person relapsing back into an addiction cycle to cope with the stress or pain. Precipitating factors can unmask an underlying propensity to develop an addictive illness in which a person may already be more predisposed to but  does not develop it until the right triggers then tip the scales over for him or her to start developing one.

Perpetuating

Perpetuating factors are factors that prolong or cause a condition to persist. Examples of such factors in addictions could be living with a family member that continues to use drugs, poor coping mechanisms, personality problems that cause someone to be unable to form long lasting relationships etc. Such perpetuating factors then cause a person to not be able to "get out" of an addiction as there are no other support systems available.

Protective

Protective Factors are factors that improve the chances of recovery from an addiction. Examples include having a supportive family, friends or having good network of support. It could also be having a stable employment, having a good marital relationship or even having early access to treatment.

Using 4 P Framework to Aid Recovery

Applying the 4P framework above would help in defining factors pertaining to the individual that aid in his or her recovery from their addiction. For instance, Let's use the hypothetical example of John who is a 45-year-old divorcee, staying alone. He has been drinking 2 bottles of rice wine daily for the past 2 years after his divorce and his mood has been pervasively low since then. He also lost his job because of his drinking and frequent absenteeism, and he recently developed a heart attack which he barely survived.

You are seeing John in the clinic and he is extremely tremulous, having last drank 24 hours ago. He Is noticeably emaciated, and he tells you that he has been having passive suicidal thoughts although he does not have active plans. His mother accompanied him for the consult and said that John is in an extremely bad physical and mental state, and she worries whether he can pull himself together. She mentioned that her husband passed away from alcohol related liver failure and she is worried John will too.

She mentioned that John still goes to church weekly, but the church pastors have expressed concern about John's condition and they have tried counselling him to no avail. She mentioned that John's elder brother has tried counselling him too and that John's children, two boys aged 18 and 16 who are under his ex-wife's custody are currently not seeing him much due to his drinking habits.

John reports drinking 2 bottles of rice wine daily starting from morning till night. He reports strong withdrawal symptoms when he doesn't drink and he has strong cravings for drinking. He does not really derive much satisfaction from drinking, and he takes a sip of his rice wine every few minutes. He cannot seem to control or stop his drinking, having tried unsuccessfully to stop many times.

Let's use the 4P framework to analyze factors affecting John's recovery.

Predisposing: John's family history of drinking. John's father also suffered from alcohol dependence, and he is likely to have strong genetic and environmental factors predisposing to drinking when he was growing up.

Precipitating factors: John's alcohol use seemed to have been triggered by his divorce and thereafter spiraled out of control.

Perpetuating factors: John's poor health, having had a heart attack lately, loss of job, poor nutrition and possibly co-morbid depression would likely contribute to him continuing to drink alcohol. Furthermore, John does not seem amenable to counselling as had been attempted by his church counsellors and elder brother.

Protective factors: John has support from his mother, elder brother and church and these are important pillars of support we can tap on for his recovery journey.

Now let's use the Addiction Equation to analyze the severity of John's Addiction.

$$\text{Severity of Addiction} = \frac{(\text{Pleasure} + \text{Urge}) \times \text{Speed}^2}{\text{Control}}$$

The variables in this equation are defined as follows:

Pleasure-Degree or magnitude of positive sensations derived Speed-Frequency of onset of a particular activity.

Urge-The desire to use a particular substance or perform a particular activity.

Control-Ability to exercise judgement and restraint in carrying out a particular activity.

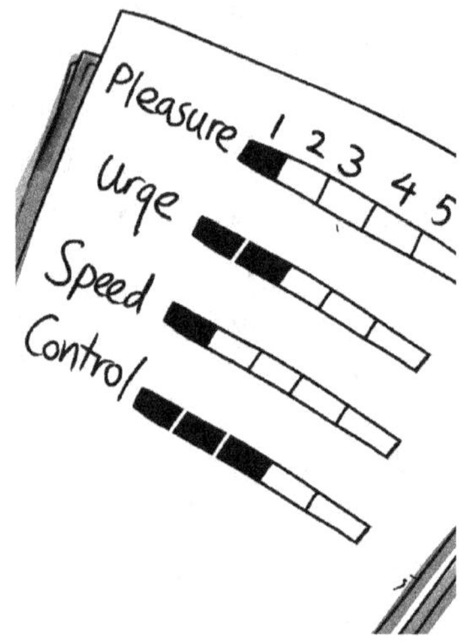

Pleasure: 1–5, where 1 is almost no pleasure, 2 is little pleasure, 3 is moderate pleasure, 4 is significantly high pleasure and 5 is very high pleasure, measured in terms of the degree or magnitude of positive sensations derived from an activity.

Urge: 1–5, where 1 is almost no urge, 2 is little urge, 3 is moderate degree of urge, 4 is significant urge and 5 is very high degree of urge, measured in terms of the desire to use a substance or perform a particular activity.

Speed: 1–5, where 1 is activity that takes place very slowly, 2 where activity is slow, 3 where activity is moderate in speed, 4 where activity is fast and 5 where the activity takes place very rapidly.

Control: 1–5, where 1 is almost no control, 2 is little control, 3 is moderate degree of control, 4 is a lot of control and 5 is absolute control over a particular activity.

2/5–25: low severity
26–100: moderate severity
101–250: high severity

For this scenario, I would quantify pleasure as 1 as John does not derive much pleasure from drinking, urge is 5 as he has strong urges to drink to relieve withdrawal symptoms, speed is 3 as he drinks every few minutes or so, not gulping down the entire bottle of rice wine immediately. Control is 1 as he has not much control over his drinking.

$$\text{Severity of addiction} = (1+5) \times 3^2/1 = 6 \times 9 = 54$$

This score of 54 is less than our earlier Heroin example in chapter 1 but more than our social media example. Again, the utility of scoring this is to help us as a gauge as to the underlying severity of John's condition but also to track his progress over time. Based on the score of 54, John likely has a moderate severity of illness and we should use this score as well as the formulation above to come up with an appropriate treatment plan for John's recovery journey as well as monitor his recovery. This will be covered in later chapters on management of addictions.

Let's use another example to see how the 4P framework can be used to analyse Samuel's recovery from Gambling Disorder.

Samuel is a patient that is on treatment for gambling disorder. He first encountered gambling in his teens during a trip overseas when he was able to enter a casino. He mentioned that since that, he had been fascinated by the idea of gambling and how people were able to make money off it. He was also fascinated by what he had seen in the casinos and how they could essentially have meals there and be entertained nonstop by different types of "gambling machines" and even play different types of table games. He viewed gambling as an easy way to make money and felt that he could make a living out of it if he was skilled enough at certain games like blackjack and baccarat.

Samuel had always been a risk taker, he liked adventure sports, rock-climbing, white water rafting etc and he was into motorbike racing later as well. He mentioned that he usually got bored with things quite quickly and was known to be impulsive as well, frequently getting into fights when he was in school, and he had even challenged his teachers to fights. Samuel started mixing with bad company early on in life and started learning how to smoke and even experimented with drugs on occasion. His parents were busy professionals who were always busy with their own work and lives. He was the youngest child in the family, having an older brother and an older sister who were more than 10 years older than him, and they didn't really talk to him much when he was growing up. None of the other family members gambled and they were all working by the time Samuel was in secondary school.

Before long, he was of legal age and started going to the casinos in Singapore to gamble. He found that time always passed much faster in the casinos and it was the one place he always found exciting and thrilling enough for him to stay hours and sometimes overnight at. Thereafter, he lost his job as a bartender due to fights at work after having had a few drinks and he started spending longer and longer hours in the casino. Before long, he was heavy in debts, having borrowed money from friends, family, and licensed moneylenders to finance his gambling. His parents have bailed him out of his debts multiple times and he had promised them that he would stop gambling but the thrill of gambling and the preoccupation with chasing his losses meant that he never managed to abstain from gambling for more than a few months in duration.

Eventually, the family took an exclusion order to ban him from the casinos and that's when he started gambling online. This was the last straw for his family who enforced the need for him to seek treatment. Whilst seeing me in the clinic, Samuel was still visibly placing bets on his phone and seemed to have poor insight into his illness. He informed me that he was still gambling every day and cannot seem to control his gambling, spending thousands of dollars on baccarat online. He was still fixated on getting his next big win and sometimes the thrill of winning money and the urge to chase losses even though these amounts were negligible compared to his debts, gave him the impetus to carry on.

Can you use the 4P framework to analyse the factors pertaining to Samuel's recovery.

Predisposing: Samuel's personality, being a risk taker, impulsive in nature. Smoking at an early age and early experimentation with drugs, neglect from family and mixing with bad company.

Precipitating: Losing his job.

Perpetuating: Seeking thrill from gambling. Repeated bailouts by family. Poor insight into gambling behaviour, gambling related cognitive distortions, poor control over gambling behaviour.

Protective: Family being supportive in his treatment.

Now let's use the Addiction Equation to analyze the severity of Samuel's Addiction.

$$\text{Severity of Addiction} = \frac{(\text{Pleasure} + \text{Urge}) \times \text{Speed}^2}{\text{Control}}$$

The variables in this equation are defined as follows:

Pleasure-Degree or magnitude of positive sensations derived
Speed-Frequency of onset of a particular activity.
Urge-The desire to use a particular substance or perform a particular activity.
Control-Ability to exercise judgement and restraint in carrying out a particular activity.

Pleasure: 1–5, where 1 is almost no pleasure, 2 is little pleasure, 3 is moderate pleasure, 4 is significantly high pleasure and 5 is very high pleasure, measured in terms of the degree or magnitude of positive sensations derived from an activity.

Urge: 1–5, where 1 is almost no urge, 2 is little urge, 3 is moderate degree of urge, 4 is significant urge and 5 is very high degree of urge, measured in terms of the desire to use a substance or perform a particular activity.

Speed: 1–5, where 1 is activity that takes place very slowly, 2 where activity is slow, 3 where activity is moderate in speed, 4 where activity is fast and 5 where the activity takes place very rapidly.

Control: 1–5, where 1 is almost no control, 2 is little control, 3 is moderate degree of control, 4 is a lot of control and 5 is absolute control over a particular activity.

2/5–25: low severity
26–100: moderate severity
101–250: high severity

For this scenario, I would quantify pleasure as 4, urge as 5, control as 1 and speed as 5.

$$\text{Addiction Severity} = 4 + 5 \times 5^2/1 = 225$$

This then signifies a high severity of addictions. For this scenario, Samuel still experiences significantly high amounts of pleasure from gambling, hoping for his next big win, hence this has been quantified as 4. He is preoccupied with chasing losses and the severe urge to chase losses together with the seemingly lack of control (still gambling on his phone whilst seeing me in clinic) made me quantify urge as 5, speed as 5 and control as 1.

The actual quantification of the above variables which then leads to the final calculated number would depend on the actual presentation of the client when you see him or her. The clinical descriptors provided in these case discussions may not accurately portray the severities of the conditions but serves as a guide on how to score using the addiction equation and helps you trend subsequently depending on the progress of the patient.

What we have described in this chapter and the focus really is on describing various elements that made Addiction a chronic illness and how we can analyse the various elements at play in any addiction pertaining to the individual so as to plan intervention strategies.

Reference

1. https://www.cnb.gov.sg/NewsAndEvents/News/Index/drugs-related-findings-from-imh-study

QUIZ TIME 4:

1. Which of the following is not an example of a chronic illness?

   a) Diabetes

   b) Hypertension

   c) Addictions

   d) Flu

2. Which of the following Ps is not part of the 4P model in conceptualizing chronic illnesses?

   a) Precipitating Factors

   b) Protective Factors

   c) Positioning Factors

   d) Predisposing Factors

3. When we talk about addictions, which term describes people who are doing well and are not in relapse of their illness?

    a) In recovery

    b) In recidivism

    c) In repentance

    d) In regression

5

NEW WORLD ADDICTIONS-"DIGITAL HEROIN"

 CHAPTER 5

This chapter is devoted to what I term new world addictions because it is indeed a brave new world that we live in. The technological advances in the recent decade have brought forth an onslaught of new digital media. These include various types of online multiplayer games, social media, gambling, pornography etc. Currently, we are also in the age of artificial intelligence, and this also brings forth new challenges and opportunities. As mentioned earlier, such new world addictions has also been termed "digital Heroin".

Most people have come to see new technological advances, including artificial intelligence as here to stay and indeed it would be remiss for anyone looking to thrive in this world not to keep themselves abreast of what is developing in this space. Caution however comes in when our Youth are exposed to some of this media whilst their brains are still developing, as they are unable to process the gamut of information that their brains are flooded with every day.

Many people have said that technology is just a vessel, that it has the potential for good and bad depending on how you use it and what you use it for. Indeed, there are a lot of truths to that as many people have found jobs which were never available before the advent of social media. For example, professional youtubers or professional E-sports players. These types of vocation only came forth with the presence of these types of social media and online gaming. Also, there are various types of influencers now being paid depending on the numbers of views they get on social media and these are legitimate professions in this day and age. Youth also use social media nowadays as a means to connect to other Youth and get their news about the events happening around the world. So indeed, there are multiple benefits through the advent of technology.

Is Social Media Addictive?

In spite of the numerous benefits that are being brought about by new technology, it is also true that many of these new forms of online digital media are inherently built to attract and keep your attention. Indeed, the longer you stay on the social media or the game, the more the developers of the platform or the game stand to gain from you. The metrics for success at any social media platform has inherently got to be the amount of time that you spend engaging on it, as the term social media implies.

One of the many criticisms about the newer social media apps is the way they generate content to match what you spend more time browsing on. This is built into their algorithms. The more time you spend on a particular subject matter or topic, the more of such material is curated and fed back to you. In a way, then the more you surf, the more you get the desired content being provided to you. Seeing a post or social media content you like generates a dopamine spike in your brain's synapses. The more dopamine spikes you receive and the faster you receive it, the more likely you are to get "hooked" onto a social media platform. Can you imagine receiving faster and faster dopamine spikes as you surf a platform designed to curate content to your liking? This is what I call digital Heroin at its very best.

Recently, Meta has announced that there will be new teen Instagram accounts with various features, such as content restrictions and messaging restrictions and also inbuilt reminders for teens to leave Instagram usage after 60 minutes of use. Why are these features important? Precisely because of what we have mentioned earlier. These help to reduce the amount of time adolescents spend on social media which in a

recent Institute of Mental Health (IMH) study (National Youth Mental Health Study initiated in 2022) has been shown to be associated with mental health symptoms. What the study found was that about 27 per cent of Youth (15–35) in Singapore reported spending more than 3 hours on social media platforms daily and these young people were more likely to have had severe or extremely severe symptoms of depression, anxiety or stress.[1]

What are some of the reasons why people spend so much time on social media? One of the reasons is as discussed above, in that social media generates content based on what you spend more time dwelling on, so as to be able to curate content that you like which would therefore "encourage" you to spend more time browsing. Another reason is that social media enables you to follow people or celebrities that you like and hence allows you to live vicariously through the lives of others.

There is also the fear of missing out in which people on social media follow their friends or colleagues just to be able to keep in the know of what their friends or families or colleagues are doing and sort of take part or be able to comment on their interesting experiences once such experiences are posted online. Without social media, one would find it difficult to keep in touch with so many people all at once all over the world. Of course, the various functions such as the ability to like a post or comment on a post also inherently makes social media activity addictive as generally people are rewarded to post more to generate "likes" in their post. This is ingrained in our biological DNA to be socially accepted and to find commonality with others.

However, there are many downsides to this in a society. Some criticisms of social media is that this makes us very superficial as a society as we only portray the good aspects of our lives on social media. It also creates a culture of comparison and may lead to unbeknownst consequences on our youth who sometimes see envy in those who have more material possessions than them.

Furthermore, I have also seen cases of online bullying on social media whereby youth report people posting nasty comments on their online posts to either discredit them or make fun of their posts. Indeed, the same IMH study mentioned above showed that about 21 per cent of Youth had been cyber bullied and that young people who had been cyber bullied were around 2x as likely to have had severe or extremely severe symptoms of depression, anxiety or stress, compared to those who had not.[1] Suffice to say that there are a lot of harms associated with online social media use and for our youth, perhaps there needs to be some form of regulation including age limit restrictions to avoid the risks associated with social media use at a young age.

Indeed, there was a recent World Health Organization report titled Health Behaviour in School-Aged Children (HBSC) 2021/22 that looked at adolescent social media use and gaming in Europe, Central Asia and Canada and this report showed that there was evidence of increasing problematic social media usage. The report recommended to strengthen measures on access and regulation for young people.[2] This is in line with recent similar announcements by Instagram to introduce Teen accounts, strengthening the message that social media use needs to be monitored carefully for our Youth. Another recent news was Australia's plans to ban social media for those under 16 years of age, a move that signals how some authorities are placing increased emphasis on the dangers of social media, especially on the developing minds of our Youth.

One of the teens that I have seen for social media problems, whom I refer to as Z, has been spending long hours, perhaps more than 10 hours a day on various social media channels, such as YouTube, Instagram and tik-tok. He compulsively searches for videos related to things he is interested in, such as gaming videos, documentaries, dance videos etc and he has subscribed to multiple channels featuring influencers that he is following. All this in the hope that he won't miss out on any interesting videos posted by these people. His obsession into surfing for such videos takes precedence over any other activities in his life and he has been missing school at times after waking up late due to using mainly YouTube late into the night. He has also over-ridden parental controls on his phone and even found a way to use the home Wi-Fi network despite the password being changed by his parents.

At school, he would always be preoccupied about what new videos have been posted by the channels he has subscribed to and he has poor concentration in class. His grades have been dropping as well and he is in danger of being retained. So, despite there being no such diagnosis of social media addiction in the DSM-5 or ICD-11 at present, I believe that cases like Z are present out there with many teens or even young adults spending a disproportionate amount of time on social media and neglecting other aspects of their lives. Whether these people suffer from an addiction remains to be seen, but this is likely if the use of the social media has caused impairment or if it has taken front and centre stage to the exclusion of other activities, i.e. Salience.

Online-Gaming

Let's go on to online video-gaming. Many of the elements in online video games also entice the gamer to spend more time gaming online. For example, being able to win items through loot boxes and level up your characters. Being able to unlock certain levels or characters if you reach a certain milestone in a gameplay or being able to dress your avatars in different clothes or costumes. These elements in gameplay bear certain resemblance to what users experience in the gambling industry, for example on jackpot machines, in which reinforcing audiovisuals are played to provide continuous feedback to the user to enrich their sensory experience and so make it more likely that they will continue gambling.

The difference is that in online gaming, these sensory experiences and these positive feedback loops are greatly amplified just purely based on the amount of sensory stimuli that is being produced. The games in the past relied on 32bit or 64bit graphic card technology whereas the games played nowadays are so complex that they need superior processing units just to be able to support the multitude of functions that the gameplay requires. With this complexity in the games, comes the ability to absorb anybody's attention and game creators are hard pressed to come up with strategies to make you spend more time on their games and spread this to others by creating virtual communities that can play the games together.

 CHAPTER 5

Let's take the case of ZX, who had seen me for problems related to online gaming. His condition was so bad that he was totally unkempt when he presented to my clinic and his parents were distraught as he was spending at that time, up to 72 hours at a stretch in LAN shops. When he saw me, he had long hair and long nails that had not been cut for a very long time and he smelt malodorous as he had not showered for many days as well. This was an extreme example of someone who had seen me for Gaming Disorder, and he was just so enthralled at gaming that he had neglected even his own personal hygiene whilst doing so. Not only had ZX neglected his own hygiene, but he was also in an extremely poor state of physical health as he had not eaten properly for several days and looked extremely malnourished. He also hadn't slept properly in a long time, as he was spending most of his time in the LAN shops. When he had disappeared for 72 hours in a row, his parents decided that this was the last straw and forcibly made him seek help.

Online Pornography

Pornography has evolved with the advent of the internet. Hardcopy magazines and explicitly printed materials are now a thing of the past. Some of the most frequented websites on the internet have been reported to be adult websites such as Pornhub and XVideos based on a Wikipedia search. This easy access to pornography is concerning as Youth who encounter such websites necessarily get drawn in with the onset of their pubertal development.

Furthermore, the rapid availability of such media along with the unrealistic depictions of the sexual encounter may lead to Youth developing unnatural and unrealistic fantasies involving sex.

Some of the media may even depict deviant types of sexual behaviour, including violence and paraphilic behaviours which may then lead to the formation of unhealthy sexual predilections later on.

During my clinical consults, I have encountered individuals, often young male adults who spent several hours of their time every day browsing internet websites for pornography. A few of them have reported to me that they subsequently suffered from erectile dysfunction and there were a few who were unable to have normal sexual intercourse with their spouses. Still some others went on to frequent commercial sex workers in order to satisfy their sexual fantasies.

This gamut of online pornography that is available and the rapid online access makes it more likely that someone will develop an addiction to pornography due to the gradual desensitization to the images seen. Indeed, it may also lead to an escalation fairly rapidly due to the various degrees of sexually explicit material available online, allowing users to move from vanilla pornography to those involving violent or even paraphilic genres due to a desensitization to the material. These then leads to unhealthy psychological concepts being formed in the Youth, pertaining to sex and this is particularly concerning.

One example of a young adult, Mr. J, who has seen me for his pornography addiction is as follows. Mr. J started surfing for online pornography in his late teens and this soon escalated to daily usage of pornography and then he started watching more and more deviant forms of pornography, initially involving some degree of violence and later on more and more extent of sadomasochism. He mentioned that this was because he could no longer get sexually aroused with just the normal forms of pornography and eventually even such violent forms of

pornography weren't enough to "excite" him. He then took to visiting commercial sex workers and even went on to demand certain of these acts he had seen online on the sexual workers, which they refused. He also suffered from erectile dysfunction as he needed to take Viagra as a young man in his prime, due to his gradual psychological desensitization to what is otherwise normal sexual behaviour. Such is the damage that watching pornography can do to a developing mind, especially with this easy online access and being potentially flooded with such numerous online material in this day and age.

Online Gambling

Is Online gambling any different from traditional forms of gambling? Gambling has taken many different forms across cultures and across generations, from horse racing, dog racing, chicken fighting, sports betting, table games in casinos, jackpot machines and now online gambling.

Online Gambling is banned in Singapore with the exception of those operated by Singapore Pools and these are for good reasons. The ease of access to online gambling if unchecked by the Gambling Regulatory Authority would mean that many people could end up squandering huge amounts of money online and this could include vulnerable young people. Indeed, many online gambling websites would offer you free tokens or credits to get you started on your gambling journey and many such websites are possible wired to ensure that you win money in the initial first few rounds to get you enticed or "hooked" onto gambling.

These are the perils of online gambling websites which are highly unregulated and served by algorithms designed to extract money from you in faster ways than traditional forms of gambling. Furthermore, in online gambling, despite feeling that you are playing the same games as in a casino, e.g. baccarat, roulette etc, what is happening is that you are actually just playing against computer algorithms designed to beat you in every way. These online games are also engineered in such a way to trap your attention through enticing imagery, sounds and using various tricks to get you to stay in the game. As such, the potential for being addicted is so much more compared to traditional forms of gambling. Furthermore, for some of these online gambling platforms, it's not so easy to claim back your money or to unsubscribe as testified by some of the patients I have treated. Usually, there is a "cooling-off" period before which you can completely get back your money or to remove yourself from the platform, making it that much harder to remove yourself from gambling online.

Take for example my patient ST who is in his 30s and started gambling online just a year ago. Within 6 months, he managed to accumulate 10k in debts and he found himself winning very big early on, enticed by the free credits and the easy wins early on in the game. However, within days of starting gambling on the online casino, he started losing hundreds of dollars and he found himself betting bigger and bigger amounts to chase back his losses. Eventually, his gambling spiralled out of control, and he was betting up to 1 thousand dollars a bet, an amount he didn't actually have but this did not matter as it was tied up to his credit card. Soon, his credit card debts escalated quite substantially, and it didn't help as he was also gambling on several websites concurrently in an effort to chase back his losses. This actually compounded the problem as the losses multiplied several folds. As his losses escalated, he started experiencing depressive symptoms and had passive suicidal thoughts. He could barely function at work as he was just thinking about how to repay his losses quickly to settle his debts. He was also gambling online whilst at work.

Such a situation would not have escalated so quickly I can imagine if the mode of gambling wasn't online and if ST wasn't able to gamble so readily on so many different websites and whilst he was at work. Despite the legal restrictions on online gambling in Singapore, some people still manage to do so through the use of virtual private networks. Again, this belies the fact that for patients who are truly addicted to online gambling, the lure to go back to gamble is so strong that they would even take risks and flout the laws.

E-Cigarettes and Vaping

It may be surprising that I am including E-Cigarettes under this chapter as a new world addiction. Whilst E-cigarettes is not an online addiction per se, it involves new technology or a new form of device that channels an old form of addiction, i.e. a new way of delivering nicotine. The mechanism of E-cigarettes and the potential of delivering higher concentrations of nicotine, especially in a manner which is more palatable to our Youth, with the vast variety of flavours and the sleek handy design, makes it so much more enticing to our Youth and young adults. Unlike traditional cigarettes with a need to light up, such E-Cigarettes or E-vaporizes are also not easy to detect, often with colourless and somewhat odourless vapours being released compared to the smoke from traditional cigarettes. These new generation E-cigarettes are becoming smaller and trendier and much more difficult to detect. Indeed, such devices have also been used to smoke other substances like Cannabis and we need to keep a watchful eye of how technology changes traditional ways of substance use.

In my clinical consults, I have come across Youth who have switched from smoking cigarettes to using E-cigarettes instead. One such example is SH, SH is a secondary school boy who had picked up cigarette smoking from his friends in school as well as from his father who was also a smoker. He was smoking up to 10 cigarettes a day and later, many of his friends switched to using E-cigarettes instead, a trend which he followed. However, he didn't completely stop smoking after starting his use of E-cigarettes, instead still smoking 2–3 cigarettes a day on top of the E-cigarette use. So essentially, SH was what we call a dual user of both traditional cigarettes and E-cigarettes, a phenomenon which is not uncommon among E-cigarette users. Despite many of the claims that E-cigarettes can help in smoking cessation, they are essentially a way of prolonging the use of nicotine. With such new technology, we are essentially transforming the way nicotine is delivered and the addiction doesn't stop. In fact, some would say that this manner of delivery becomes more palatable to our youth, many of whom would not have been enticed to smoke in the first place.

 CHAPTER 5

Are Digital Devices Harmful

This topic is perhaps one of the more controversial topics as far as parents are concerned. In light of the recent media attention given to personal learning devices covered in the Straits Times article titled "Personal learning devices in schools-Boon or Bane?" on 20 Oct 2024, there has been much attention given to the topic of having learning devices such as iPads as learning aids in schools.

Indeed, during my talks with educators in schools, one of the more common questions asked is if handphones or other types of digital devices should be banned in schools. This is a very polarizing topic as there are some people who feel that digital devices have a place in learning whilst some people feel that there are too many distractions available on such devices and it is hard for students to focus on the studying and learning if there are so many possible notifications being given by such devices.

My opinion is similar and whilst I share the view that some device time is necessary for learning in the digital age, there is much danger in allowing the permissibility of having such devices anywhere, anytime in the classroom. The reason is simple, such devices are inherently not bad or evil but the vast amount of possible notifications through the numerous number of applications now, via social media, email notifications and other seemingly innocuous apps can really place a stranglehold on anyone's attention.

Hence, we need to carefully decide if having such devices in the classroom has more benefits than the possible harms it introduces. We also need to decide at what age it is appropriate for students to start using such personal learning devices as starting its usage at a young age may then expose youth to other sorts of dangers such as online pornography etc. Perhaps, what is then a suitable alternative is to greatly restrict the use of such devices to a minimum to what's essential for learning and then highly regulate its use in the classroom setting. This involves careful planning of the curriculum and inputs from educators as to what modules can be done offline and what modules need to be done online so as to determine if the devices need to be in the students' hands during that particular session.

As far as possible, I would advocate that most of the time, during school going hours, students should not have the devices on hand where possible to allow them to fully engage in the school curriculum content. At least, this should be till upper secondary level when the brain is more matured to be able to filter out content effectively and where greater responsibility in the use of such devices can be expected.

Also furthermore, the use of such digital devices need to be supervised to ensure that Youth are not using them for harmful online content such as pornography and if necessary parents and teachers need to be mindful of the impact of social media use on the developing adolescent brain, potentially exposing the youth early to online bullying and an unhealthy comparison with others based on what material possessions they have. This use of digital devices must also be carefully balanced with outdoor activities to ensure that the development of our Youth's physical health is also taken into consideration and that they are not overly stimulated by the digital devices. In short, balance is everything when it comes to our Youth.

Telescoping

When it comes to addiction, there are certain phenomena worth mentioning. One of which is telescoping, in which an addiction which starts off slowly suddenly escalates in severity fairly rapidly. This is often described for female alcoholics when the intensity of drinking which was once mild can suddenly become severe very rapidly without much warning. In addition to the above, I have also observed this trend in terms of digital addictions. Some parents whom I have spoken to have told me how rapidly their adolescent children have become glued onto their digital devices after they were given said devices as presents. There was often an element of regret and many a times, the interval between the introduction of such devices to problematic use and formation of an addiction can be as short as a few weeks in duration.

This rapid acceleration of the intensity of an addiction or the rapid development of a problematic behaviour when there was none before is what I have clinically observed for some digital addictions such as online gaming and also gambling. This is hardly surprising as earlier in the chapter, we talked about how the algorithms dictating gameplay are inherently designed to capture your attention as much as possible. The rewarding features of such gameplay and the different permutations they do so with the audiovisual stimulation and the introduction of enticing elements like loot boxes, means that the player has little reason for diverting time away from the engaging gameplay. Before long, the addiction has set in and it becomes that much more difficult to remove these devices. Indeed, many parents lament how they have had to endure temper tantrums, meltdowns and sometimes even frank violent behaviours from their adolescent children, when attempting to remove these digital gadgets.

One example is with a patient by the name of W. W was brought to see me by his parents when he was in secondary one. Then he had already started stealing his parents credit

cards to purchase in-game items so as to enhance his characters in the games. The situation was so bad that the parents had raked up thousands of dollars in credit card bills. W's gaming started when he was in primary 6, just slightly shy of one year before he

started using his parent's credit cards to purchase the online in-game items. He was spending close to 13 hours a day playing the game online and he was also gaming into the wee hours of the night.

As a result, he frequently got up late and at times even missed school. Needless to say, his grades deteriorated, from being a top student in class to then being at the bottom of the class. The irony was that he was given the handphone as a present for performing well in his PSLE. Shortly after receiving the handphone, he had downloaded multiple applications, including various games such as Fortnite and League of Legends and also various social media apps such as Instagram and tik-tok. Within a month of receiving the hand phone, he had spent so much time on his new device, that this grades in school started dropping and he was noticeably more tired in school. Within 4 months, his parents were called to a parent-teachers meeting and it was later revealed that his stealing of his parent's credit cards began 6 months after receiving the phone.

Such is the nature of telescoping, a rapid worsening of the addiction, that makes such online addiction even more concerning especially when the right milieu occurs for it to happen.

Device Induced Attention Deficit

This is another controversial topic but which I would like to highlight. Much of this is gained from personal insights having spoken to parents and indeed counsellors who have treated children who are constantly glued in on their devices. Some parents have complained that their children have become highly distractible and there are even some spouses who have also lamented that their better halves have been become "ADHD", always attending to their phones and missing out on conversations.

Is this device induced ADHD legitimate? Again, this will be controversial as we are saying that ADHD can have origins at a later age in life as opposed to the traditional teaching of it being a developmental condition with its roots in early childhood. However, from research into substance use, we are aware that patients with substance use can show ADHD symptoms later on in life, hence if we apply the same logic to gaming and other device use, the same outcome can be expected.

How do our digital devices induce ADHD? It is actually very plausible, we all know there is some degree of neuroplasticity even as we progress towards adulthood. With this neuroplasticity, as we constantly get inundated with messages or notifications from the various applications, our brains get hijacked with such notifications when we may be busy with other things. This then prunes our neuronal circuits and makes us more easily distractible as we have to adapt to all these constant disruptions induced by the notifications on our apps.

This is indeed a pandemic in the making and we need to be careful of this emerging trend. Of course, further research also needs to be made in this area especially with the advent of newer and newer social media platforms that constantly are made to absorb our attention.

One example of this is YS, a teenager who had seen me for problems related to social media use. She has been referred by her parents and her school due to emotional problems after being bullied by her friends in school, especially on social media, where people were calling her names and posted nasty comments on her Facebook page. She was highly distractible in class, constantly checking on her social media pages to ensure that she replied to every comment that was made. It took a toll on her mental health and she was also verbally teased in school. This made her parents consider switching schools for her. However, prior to being exposed to social media, YS was performing well in primary and secondary school and was not so highly distractible in class. What was also evident was that she was extremely restless in the clinic on seeing me, constantly checking her phone and not able to attend fully to the conversation with me.

Despite all the dangers of the online world that we have discussed in this chapter, it is highly evident that this is here to stay and we need to be aware how to navigate this brave new world with our Youth.

Our Education Minister, Minister Chan has recently launched the Parenting for Wellness Toolbox for Parents and inside this toolkit, there are useful topics on helping children navigate the digital age.[3] I would like to encourage all parents to use this as there are some useful infographics that provide useful information to parents on how to make the online world safer.

Balance is Everything

Despite all that has been said about the online world, there are some notable benefits and studies have also shown benefits on gaming such as improved executive functioning and improved development in certain regions of the brain. Hence, the essence is that balance between online and offline activities is important and the brain needs to be developed in totality, not neglecting one area of development for another. Having time spent outdoors, with family and with friends in their physical presence is essential to navigating life in general and ensuring holistic development of our Youth. Family can institute screen time restrictions and have dedicated zones and times where devices are forbidden. Parents must also abide by such rules so that Youth can model after such behaviours. It would also be helpful for parents to check in time to time on what their children are doing online and to monitor for any harmful activities such as watching of pornography. This then involves appropriate conversations with Youth about the dangers of the online community and what to look out for.

References

1. Teo, J. (2024, 19 September). Key takeaways from IMH's National Youth Mental Health Study. The Straits Times. https://www.straitstimes.com/singapore/health/key-takeaways-from-imh-s-national-youth-mental-health-study

2. Boniel-Nissim M, Marino C, Galeotti T, Blinka L, Ozoliņa K, Craig W et al. A focus on adolescent social media use and gaming in Europe, central Asia and Canada. Health Behaviour in School-aged Children international report from the 2021/2022 survey. Volume 6. Copenhagen: WHO Regional Office for Europe; 2024: CC BY-NC-SA 3.0 IGO.

3. https://www.digitalforlife.gov.sg/learn/resources/all-resources/parenting-for-wellness

QUIZ TIME 5:

1. What does telescoping refer to?

    a) Rapid improvement in addiction symptoms

    b) Rapid worsening of addiction symptoms

    c) Rapid stabilisation of an addiction

    d) A period of remission in addiction symptoms

2. What areas of online use can potentially be harmful to Youth?

    a) Online Gaming

    b) Online Gambling

    c) Online pornography

    d) All of the above

3. The following are some useful strategies to help Youth navigate the use of digital devices except.

   a) Dedicated time spent outdoors on physical activities

   b) Having conversations about what Youth are engaging in online

   c) Allowing Youth unrestricted use of the internet

   d) Having tech free zones such as during mealtimes

6

SLOW THINGS DOWN

This next half of the book focusses on things we can do to tackle or manage an addiction starting from simple things you can do for yourself.

If we go back to the addiction equation, the severity of the addiction relies heavily on how fast or the speed of using a particular substance or in performing a particular type of activity, since Speed is squared in the equation.

$$\text{Severity of Addiction} = \frac{(\text{Pleasure} + \text{Urge}) \times \text{Speed}^2}{\text{Control}}$$

So one of the best things that someone can do to control an addiction once it is formed, is to slow things down.

Slowing down means taking a moment to appreciate the things around you, to be mindful of what goes on around you, to be living in the present, instead of rushing from one thing to another. In this day and age, there are always things to do. Speed then perhaps is the driving force behind many of the addictions we see today. What do I mean by that?

As we have seen earlier in chapter 3 on theories behind addictions, there are essentially 2 competing forces behind an addiction. The first one is the very basal, limbic system driven impulsive drive towards an addiction, whereas the second competing force is the regulatory control exerted largely by the frontal cortex of the brain, inhibiting such basal primitive drives.

Speed is a modulating factor between these two competing forces, in which the faster an activity is occurring, the more it takes then for the frontal lobe to be able to inhibit the basal drives as the energy and focus needed to "tame" down such drives is largely dependent on the frequency of such activity.

Essentially, the brain is not wired to receive so much stimulus in such a short amount of time and can be "overloaded" if there is too much stimulus. Let's explore the role of speed further below.

Speed of Substance Use

Take for example the case of a heroin user who has been chasing Heroin. First he or she starts with one straw of Heroin every day, then goes on to two straws and finally to a bag of Heroin. However after a few weeks, even a bag a day doesn't deliver the "high" anymore. What happens then, he or she then takes to injecting Heroin into the veins so that the effect of Heroin reaches the brain more expediently. Gradually, even injecting into the veins doesn't give the user enough "high" anymore or the veins become hardened after prolonged injecting. What happens then? The user then resorts to injecting Heroin into the femoral artery, also known as the "highway" for even more expedient action of heroin on the brain. This need for faster and faster "hits" from the Heroin then possibly results in overdose deaths from reaching the toxic cumulative dose more rapidly.

The above example portrays how as an addiction progresses, there is a need to obtain a "high" faster and faster so as to satisfy the user. Addressing the need for this speed is vital when tackling any form of addiction. Just merely slowing down the using of Heroin may in fact save the person's life by reducing the risk of overdose toxicity. This applies similarly to other drugs of abuse.

So, in the above example, one way to reduce the Speed part of the equation pertaining to substance use is to alter the route of administration. If a user changes from intravenous use to smoking Heroin for instance, the speed of activation of the pleasure receptors in the brain would have reduced quite substantially, thereby helping to reduce the severity of the addiction.

Take for example, my patient ZY, he is a person who has used Heroin and also Subutex in the past, currently he is in remission from drug use. Whilst he was still actively using Heroin, he had developed such severe dependence that he was chasing up to 5 straws of Heroin a day. When he no longer managed to achieve the high from chasing Heroin, he decided to start injecting Heroin into his veins, first his hand veins, then his leg veins and eventually he tried using the veins in his neck. Thereafter, the veins in his bodies hardened and he was unable to find any more veins to inject Heroin into. He then resorted to injecting Heroin into his femoral artery (the "highway"), which gave him such an immediate high and which was so dangerous that he had almost overdosed on Heroin on a couple of occasions. Not only did he almost die from the effects of Heroin from direct administration into an artery, he also developed an infection of his groin, which thereafter became what we term a septic emboli, in which bacteria seeded into his bloodstream and he needed to be admitted to the intensive care unit for further treatment. All this in an effort to obtain faster and more intense "highs" from Heroin.

Speed Pertaining to Social Media

Let's take another example, this time the example of social media. A person goes to a social media application that supplies him feeds of his friends perhaps posting once every few days. Then he chances upon another social media application that not only shows feeds from his friends, but also shows feeds from news outlets and celebrities he follows. The feeds come up faster than the old application because it allows him to follow more people and the posts are mostly pictures rather than words which take a long time to read. This same person then comes upon another social media application, this time the application not just shows him posts from his friends and those he follows but also random posts curated to his liking. This application provides mainly short videos as posts rather than pictures and he is allowed to swipe up and down to go to the next post at his control, each post curating content to his likes based on the length of time he has spent on similar posts. Does this sound familiar? How many of us can relate to this experience?

The above example shows how users gravitate towards social media applications that provide faster and faster positive feedback for them, through their ability to engage and interact with the user, curating content and allowing faster and faster posts to the user and increasing the speed of such interactions.

Nowadays among teens, the fear of missing out is very real. As mentioned earlier in the chapter on digital addictions, I have a patient Z who has been spending long hours, perhaps more than 10 hours a day on various social media channels, such as YouTube, Instagram and tik-tok. He compulsively searches for videos related to things he is interested in, such as gaming videos, documentaries, dance videos etc and he has subscribed to multiple channels featuring influencers that he is following. All this in the hope that he won't miss out on any interesting videos posted by these people. His obsession into surfing for such videos takes precedence over any other activities in his life and he has been missing school at times after waking up late due to using mainly YouTube late into the night. He has also over-ridden parental controls on his phone and even found a way to use the home Wi-Fi network despite the password being changed by his parents.

At school, he would always be preoccupied about what new videos have been posted on the channels he has subscribed to, and he has poor concentration in class. His grades have been dropping as well and he is danger of being retained.

When he initially started surfing for videos, it was interesting that he could watch full length videos of up to an hour when it came to interesting videos that he liked. However, as time went on, he found his attention span waning and he gravitated towards shorter and shorter videos. He also tended to move on from one video to another quickly over time, scrolling through multiple videos in a short amount of time. He particularly found Tik Tok and Instagram videos fairly enticing as they tended to offer short videos curated to his liking. This annoyed his parents a little as he would play the videos loudly over his phone and they noticed how he was switching from one video to another quickly and this interrupted their watching of the TV in the living room. As this scenario demonstrated, as an addiction develops, there is a tendency to gravitate towards faster and faster hits of self-gratification. The encounter with one interesting video that excites the user gives a hit of dopamine. The more interesting videos are watched in a shorter amount of time, the more dopaminergic surges are experienced, and this keeps the momentum going for the user. So instead of watching many short videos in a short amount of time, perhaps one harm reduction strategy is to watch one full length interesting movie to the end. This could "re-train" and unwire the damage done from doom-scrolling.

Speed Pertaining to Gambling

Next let's take the example of gambling. Imagine a gambler who starts off gambling at physical casinos and plays baccarat. He has to wait for the dealer to deal the cards to him and his speed of betting is limited by the speed of gameplay and how fast the cards are dealt. However, he chances upon an online casino. Whilst visiting this online casino, he realizes that the games played here are much faster, each game only takes a few seconds as the cards are dealt so fast that he barely has time to process before the next game starts. This is because the software just relies on an algorithm to "deal" cards. He starts to lose money and each time that he loses money, he proceeds to place the next bet faster and faster so as to recoup the losses. At the end of one hour, he has played hundreds of games, something he would not have been able to do in a physical casino.

Again, in the above example, we see how speed has resulted in the person getting more and more entrenched in the act of gambling and how slowing down conversely is going to help in his or her addiction and reducing his losses quite substantially.

An Addictive Personality

There are some patients that I have seen in my clinic whom I will term as having an addictive personality. These patients tend to have a variety of traits that make them jump from one addiction to another. Generally, they tend to have short attention spans, are impulsive in nature, tend to be thrill-seekers and need instant gratification from things. Whilst some of these patients may have attention deficit hyperactivity disorder, very often I find that clinically they do not meet the full criteria for ADHD and instead demonstrate certain facets of the illness, not enough to make a diagnosis. An example is a patient Mr XS, he has been having frequent problems with authority since young and was deemed to be a troublemaker in school and at work. He enjoyed rollers coasters and experimented with drugs when he was young. He first got exposed to alcohol during national service and shortly later became dependent on it. He later picked up smoking as well and said he started taking stimulants like ecstasy whilst out partying with friends. He mentioned that he felt more refreshed and energised after taking stimulants and that alcohol helped him "wind-down" after taking stimulants. Thereafter, he was arrested for taking stimulants and after coming out of the drug rehabilitation centre, he had switched to using benzodiazepines and Ritalin instead, becoming addicted to both. Ritalin is a stimulant medication used for ADHD treatment. Mr XS has what I believe to be an addictive personality as evidenced by him easily developing different types of addictions. Although this term is sometimes frowned upon and is not a proper clinical diagnosis, I feel that there is some value in helping to identify such patients who are at risk of addictions and in possibly helping to tailor intervention strategies for them accordingly, helping them understand the value of slowing things down and not be fixated on instant gratification.

Kindling

What happens in the brain, when someone repeatedly does an activity which provides positive feedback almost immediately? This process becomes self-reinforcing and almost akin to kindling, in which once a spark ignites, a whole chain of reactions is sparked off, causing multiple centres in the brain to light up at once, which then subsequently reinforces the initial spark that triggers it. Ultimately, what this leads to is a fired-up brain which is very difficult to calm down. This type of self-reinforcing positive feedback is almost akin to an epileptic process and leads to repeated firing of neurons in the reward pathway. The speed of activation of neurons is thus a function of the addictiveness of any drug of behaviour and the imperative here is to slow the brain down, dousing it with water if you will, to calm the overheated reward pathway.

How then do we get someone to slow down. It's not entirely that easy. Once someone is addicted to using a substance or a particular behaviour, the natural tendency is to do that act faster and faster so as to obtain the "high" or the pleasurable sensation faster and faster. This is where certain techniques come in, for example mindfulness training or meditation.

Mindfulness

What is mindfulness and how does it work? Mindfulness is a type of meditation in which the person gets in tune with his bodily sensations and feelings and learns how to "observe them" without

passing any judgement. This type of meditation takes the person away from the distractions that come from random thoughts and helps the person focus on the here and now instead.

Practitioners of mindfulness will tell you that during the sessions, they go into a state of heightened relaxation and of being in touch with their various sensations, sight, smell, touch, hearing etc. This state of focus gives them clarity and allows them to observe what goes on around them or in their "mind's eye" and also allows them to use their breathing to regulate their emotions.

Indeed, there are various health benefits to mindfulness as it tends to reduce the overactivity of the sympathetic nervous system and activates the parasympathetic nervous system. For someone with addictions, this then helps to reduce the impulsivity of that individual who practices mindfulness and helps him or her regulate his urges or cravings better, to be able to better tolerate the discomfort and also deal with psychological pain better.

Of course, there are other ways to slow the human body down. Mindfulness is only one of them. Other ways or regulating our own internal rhythms could come in the form of exercise, deep breathing techniques etc.

Effective Emotional Regulation

One of the most common reasons why people relapse to drug use is as a means of coping with stress or when there are emotional upheavals in that person's life. Such is the importance of having the ability to emotionally regulate to maintain calmness internally and to regulate our own biorhythms. The ability to emotionally regulate to "slow down" our internal rhythms can come about through mindfulness or meditation; it can also come about through appreciating who we are as a person and how we relate to others.

Generally, emotional regulation refers to our ability to maintain a state of homeostasis in our internal milieu, not veering too much from one emotional state to another. This then keeps us in a relatively calm state and prevents a person with addiction from impulsively using drugs as a means to cope. Through understanding ourselves and how we respond to stress or triggers and how we relate to others, we can find better ways of managing this relationship internally within ourselves and with others.

Most people suffering from addictions have difficulties managing or regulating their emotions and "use" their addictions as a way of managing their difficult internal states. Once the person with addictions is able to gain mastery over their internal milieu, then it becomes easier to prevent relapses into drug or alcohol use or for that matter, any other forms of addiction. Of course, emotional regulation is like a muscle that needs training much like any other physical training programme and the more we practice regulating our emotions, the more proficient we become at it. It takes patience and a willingness to understand ourselves and how we can better relate to others.

No Short Cuts and No Easy Way Out

One common distinction between patients that I have seen who have relapsed to addiction versus those that stay in sobriety is that patients in the former group often look for quick solutions to their addictions. There is often a low threshold for distress tolerance and these patients who relapse frequently are often those that also tend to look for quick relief from their problems or symptoms. An example being a patient I've seen who has developed multiple addictions, moving from one addiction to another, initially starting off with Heroin, then later using benzodiazepines to cope with the symptoms after coming off Heroin and finally later turning to alcohol to cope with the distressing symptoms after coming off benzodiazepines.

The usage of these drugs, one after another, to cope with distressing feelings and symptoms instead of working on underlying psychological and emotional issues, is a quick "fix" and as with all quick fixes, there is often no permanent solution being offered, instead just prolonging the illness and often making it easy to slip into another relapse. Instead, the best option for managing an addiction is taking the time and perhaps patience to learn the skills necessary for managing distress and being able to tolerate the discomfort that comes with it, instead of relying on quick pharmacological solutions from drugs or medications. Hence the role of mindfulness and various other cognitive strategies that will be covered later in the subsequent chapter on management of addictions. Of course, medications do have their role in maintenance of abstinence but more of as a supportive treatment rather than being the mainstay of the approach.

QUIZ TIME 6:

1. What is Kindling?

    a) An activity that reinforces itself through positive feedback

    b) An activity that results in negative feedback to discourage that same behaviour

    c) Any activity that causes burnout

    d) An activity that results in anger

2. What is homeostasis?

    a) A state of chaos

    b) A state of inner turmoil

    c) A stable internal milieu

    d) A state of decreased activity

3. Which of the following is not an effect of mindfulness?

    a) Heightened relaxation

    b) Increased anxiety

    c) Reduced tension in the body

    d) Greater clarity and focus

7

HOW TO MANAGE AN ADDICTION?

 CHAPTER 7

This next section is devoted to how we can manage and treat an addiction. In the earlier section, we already talked about one strategy in particular to slow things down. This is the technique of mindfulness. However to manage an addiction in its entirety requires more than just management of speed. Let's revisit the addiction equation again.

$$\text{Severity of Addiction} = \frac{(\text{Pleasure} + \text{Urge}) \times \text{Speed}^2}{\text{Control}}$$

The variables in this equation are:

Pleasure-Degree of pleasure derived from an activity.
Speed-Frequency of onset of a particular activity.
Urge-The desire to use a particular substance or perform an activity.
Control-Ability to exercise judgement and restraint in carrying out a particular activity.

The following scales are as defined:

Pleasure: 1–5, where 1 is almost no pleasure, 2 is little pleasure, 3 is moderate pleasure, 4 is significantly high pleasure and 5 is very high pleasure, measured in terms of the degree or magnitude of positive sensations derived from an activity.

Urge: 1–5, where 1 is almost no urge, 2 is little urge, 3 is moderate degree of urge, 4 is significant urge and 5 is very high degree of urge, measured in terms of the desire to use a substance or perform a particular activity.

Speed: 1–5, where 1 is activity that takes place very slowly, 2 where activity is slow, 3 where activity is moderate in speed, 4 where activity is fast and 5 where the activity takes place very rapidly.

Control: 1–5, where 1 is almost no control, 2 is little control, 3 is moderate degree of control, 4 is a lot of control and 5 is absolute control over a particular activity.

In terms of the equation, the maximum score that can be derived is

$$(5 + 5) \times 5^2/1 = 250$$

The minimum score that can be derived is

$$(1 + 1) \times 1^2/5 = 2/5$$

So the range is from 2/5 to 250, when we quantify the severity of an addiction.

As can be seen from this equation, the other variables of pleasure, urge and control also come into play. We have already explored the impact of speed and how to moderate this in the earlier chapter. What then helps to moderate the other variables in the equation? Let us explore each one in turn.

Pleasure

The first variable is Pleasure. Pleasure is defined as the degree of positive sensations derived from a particular substance or activity. To reduce the "Pleasure" in this equation is to reduce the amount or degree of pleasure derived from the substance or behaviour. "Pleasure" is very biological in nature and mostly driven by the properties of the substance or behaviour and its effects on our bodies. To reduce the pleasure derived from a particular substance or behaviour usually involves blocking the effects of that substance or activity on our bodies or reducing its effects through external manipulation of the properties of the substance or the way it interacts with our bodies.

An example could be the use of medications to block the effects of Heroin on the body for instance. One such medication that is used is Naltrexone, a long acting opioid antagonist that blocks the effects of opioids on the Mu-opioid receptor in the body. Such medications effectively block out the effects of Heroin as it blocks the binding of Heroin to the particular receptor that it is designed to act on. Naltrexone has also been used to reduce the pleasure from drinking alcohol and some people use the so-called Sinclair method of taking Naltrexone just before a drinking session, to reduce the satiation from drinking so as to avoid binge drinking episodes.

Instead of relying on medications to reduce or block the effects of a particular substance or behaviour on the brain, the user is also able to manipulate the properties of the substance for instance prior to consuming it, hence reducing the desired effects. An example could be diluting the Heroin to a greater extent prior to the injection for instance or diluting the whiskey with more mixers prior to drinking it. This then reduces the concentration of the particular substance and reduces the effect of the substance on the brain, hence reducing the positive feedback that comes from it and reducing the "Pleasure" in the equation. This is part of the harm reduction advice that clinicians sometimes give to patients who are heavy drinkers, to avoid the effects of binge drinking and also to reduce the chances of getting intoxicated with alcohol.

I have a patient, Mr Z, who has seen me for many years, and he has been diagnosed with alcohol use disorder. He enjoys drinking red wine, and he is in the creative industry. He mentioned that he would usually go out with friends after work for a drink or two and he also enjoys drinking wine at home with his wife. He has a wine fridge at home and he has about 50 bottles of wine on any occasion. The problem with his drinking is that once he drinks past a certain level, usually 3 glasses of red wine, he would be unable to control how much he would drink and subsequently ends up intoxicated. Mr Z has tried several treatments in the past but none seemed to work well for him and he found the Sinclair method of using Naltrexone useful.

He mentioned that by taking Naltrexone before the drinking episode, he did not experience such a high after drinking and was able to better control the amount of red wine that he drank. He noticed that he was able to avoid binge drinking episodes and has stopped getting intoxicated after going out drinking with friends. He also did not want to have to take Naltrexone everyday as he mentioned that he wouldn't drink daily and averaged 3x a week. Hence, he would only prefer to take Naltrexone 3x a week as he mentioned that he did experience some mild side effects after taking the medication.

Hence, reducing pleasure from otherwise addictive substances would go a long way towards reducing the reinforcement effects and possibly help in providing better control of the drinking as well.

Urge

Now, lets' look at the next variable in the equation, that of "urge". How do we reduce the desire to use a substance or

perform a particular activity. These could involve either therapy or medications. We talked earlier about kindling and the positive reinforcing nature of substances. Part of this process involves conditioning in which certain physiological and psychological responses are triggered when substances are being used. Therapy then employs a process to desensitize or decondition the brain such that it is no longer so fired up by the substances when they are being used. This could involve pairing up the usage of the substance with a negative stimulus for instance, otherwise known as aversion therapy. An example could be to show to a person a picture of a badly fibrosed liver and pictures of alcohol together.

This could also involve the use of medications to reduce the urge or cravings to use particular substances or perform particular behaviours. An example is when Naltrexone is used which reduces the cravings for alcohol or for certain behavioral addictions like gambling. Other medications, such as Selective Serotonin Reuptake Inhibitors (SSRIs) have also been used off label to reduce the urges to gamble and indeed for compulsive sexual behavioural disorders as well. Still other medications like Bupropion have been used to reduce the urge to smoke. Indeed, there are many ways to reduce cravings for substances and even behavioural addictions through therapy and medications and this has been employed quite successfully in various treatment programmes.

I have a patient Miss Z, who has chronic schizophrenia and smokes up to 2 packets of cigarettes in a day. She mentions having strong cravings to smoke throughout the day and will smoke one stick of cigarette every half an hour. When I prescribed her the medication Varenicline, she said that her cravings for cigarettes abated and she was able to resist smoking and after using Varenicline for 6 months, she was able to stop smoking completely. The stronger the cravings, the more effective the anti-cravings medications would be.

Control

We have talked about "speed" earlier in the chapter on slowing things down, so perhaps we next go on to "control". How do we enable better control or gain mastery over our addictive behaviours. This mostly involves Cognitive behavioural techniques, and we will cover them in more detail here.

Cognitive Behavioural Therapy

Cognitive behavioural therapy as the name suggests, deals with cognitions and behaviours in an individual. Cognitions refers to the way we think and the way we think affects the way we feel which subsequently affects the way we act, which are our behaviours. When a person who is addicted is exposed to a stimulus, for example, the sight of another user injecting drugs, certain thoughts are triggered in the person. These thoughts that immediately arise are called automatic thoughts and are our inner voices that respond to the situation. For example, in this case, the person may be thinking immediately, "this is bad for me, I will take drugs as I cannot withstand the cravings". These negative automatic thoughts then lead to negative feelings of inadequacy and poor self-worth, which may then spiral into actual drug using behaviours. An example of such a flow of events is as below.

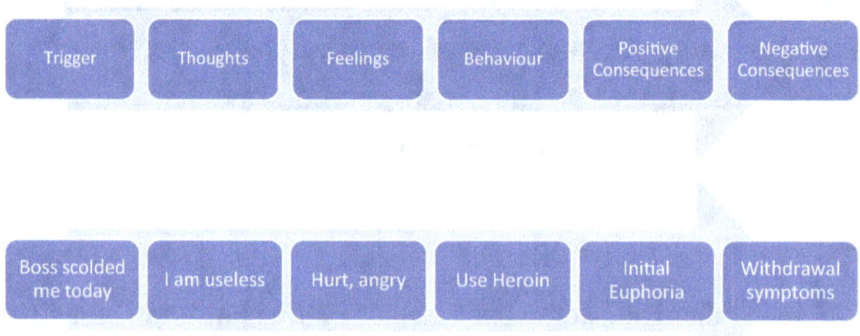

Schemas

After the initial automatic thoughts are formed, then comes an organization of such thoughts based on the underlying schema. A schema is the pattern of thoughts that an individual has based on his underlying beliefs, values and preferences. How a patient then acts upon the initial automatic thoughts is dependent on his underlying schemas, what his or her value systems place emphasis on. These schemas are often shaped by his or her environment and experiences growing up.

What therapy hopes to achieve is then to modify these thought patterns or schemas in the hope that the patient is then better able to resist the natural automatic thoughts and negative emotions which then result in him or her giving in to his cravings. This can be done through various ways, for instance, substituting negative thoughts with healthier ones and challenging underlying assumptions. I will explain more in detail below.

For instance, supposing the initial automatic thoughts are "I will surely relapse back to drugs now", cognitive behavioural therapy could involve substituting these thoughts with "I am strong enough to resist taking drugs". Of course, substituting these negative thoughts with more positive ones takes time and practice, which is why CBT involves repetition and homework to be done away from the actual consult time with the therapist. Besides substituting the automatic thoughts, the therapy also involves challenging or changing the underlying schemas.

To challenge underlying schemas requires much more work as schemas are built up over time. However, this aspect is often the more sustaining work of CBT as the effects are often longer lasting. An example of a schema that could have developed over time in this case could be the individual believing that he is inherently unable to resist the urge to use drugs as he is "weak by nature". This type of unhelpful schema really eats away at the individual's ability to fight off any cravings or use helpful coping strategies.

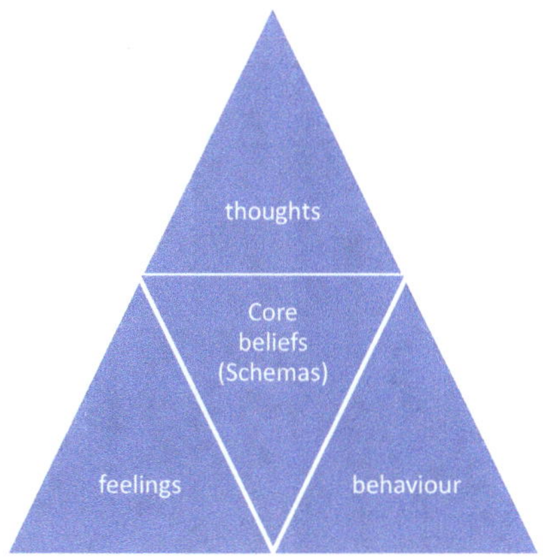

CBT then seeks to replace such unhealthy thought patterns with more positive ones that seek to build on the individual's resolve and resilience.

An example of such a schema could be, "I am a fighter and have enough coping resources to prevent relapsing into drug use." However, changing underlying schemas, as opposed to changing negative automatic thoughts, usually takes more time. This is easy to appreciate as much effort is needed to change schemas. Schemas as explained, are shaped by the environment and experiences of the person growing up, hence they take long to form. This also means that they will take an equivalent if not longer amount of time to undo. Usually, to change someone's schema requires many sessions of CBT and resolve on the part of the person to do the homework that is involved. However, once the schema is sufficiently changed, then the person can properly exert mastery or control over his underlying thoughts and the way he or she reacts to triggers to use drugs.

This diagram below depicts a possible change in the emotions and behaviours that follow once negative automatic thoughts have been substituted for healthier ones.

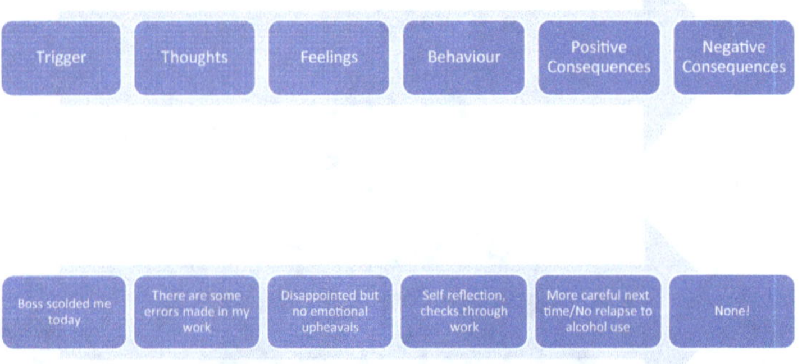

Hopefully this chapter has explained clearly how the different variables of pleasure, urge and control can be targeted in terms of treatment to ameliorate the severity of any addiction. Each of the variables mentioned here can be moderated with the help of various pharmacological or psychological treatments and even social support and hence helping to reduce the severity of the addiction. The role of speed in the equation has been covered in the preceding chapter and the role of mindfulness has been discussed on how to manage that as well.

QUIZ TIME 7:

1. What are schemas?

    a) Pattern of thoughts based on underlying beliefs, values and preferences

    b) Negative automatic thoughts

    c) Personality traits

    d) Cognitive distortions

2. What does Cognitive behavioural therapy involve?

    a) Challenging unhealthy thoughts

    b) Homework

    c) Replacing unhealthy thoughts with positive ones

    d) All of the above

3. What type of medications are not used in the management of addictions?

    a) Medications to reduce cravings

    b) Medications to help relieve withdrawal symptoms

    c) Medications that reduce the pleasurable sensations after taking the substance of abuse.

    d) Medications that induce anxiety

8

BE KIND (TO YOURSELF AND OTHERS)

This chapter is perhaps the most important chapter in this book. Very often, having an addiction is a very private problem. Most patients don't seek treatment and the few who do, often keep it to themselves. The reason for this, is that there is a lot of shame and embarrassment and often guilt pertaining to having this illness. The stigma behind having an addiction is very real. In fact, when people seek treatment from me, they often have to get past 2 stigmas. The first stigma is the stigma of having a mental illness and the next stigma is that of having an addiction. That same stigma is further amplified when family members reject patients due to their addictions and then patients are left having to fend for their own.

When I speak to other psychiatrists, it is often a sensing that very many do not fully comprehend what having an addiction really is about. Often, the default rates in clinic are high and the treatment outcomes are not very good. Even amongst subspeciality psychiatric services, there are some that will exclude patients with an active substance or alcohol use from  the services, citing that having an active alcohol or substance use will complicate the assessment. Whilst there are indeed sometimes good reasons for doing so, especially when substance use may cloud the underlying diagnosis and treatment, often, I struggle to understand why patients with addictions are excluded from some of these services. Many patients with addictions do suffer from co-morbid mental illness and sometimes they may be the ones that would paradoxically benefit most from these specialised services.

Many times, it's also hard to understand why you would expect the same outcomes for people with addictions, knowing that the condition is very intractable and there is no "cure" to speak of. People with addictions struggle with recovery every single day. There are so many factors at play in someone's recovery from an addiction, including his social environment and it is as much a medical disease as it is a social one. The balance of factors must weigh heavily in the person's favour for him or her not to relapse into an addiction on any given day. This could mean anything from having a good night's rest to going to a stable home at the end of a work shift.

Again, we are not saying that patients with addictions always have it bad for them. There are indeed many inspiring recovery stories and I have always found it heartening working in this field because of the numerous patients that I have treated who have managed their addiction successfully. The difficult part for many patients is that there is still a misunderstanding of what they are going through despite the scientific advances in the understanding of addictions.

The hard truth is that all of us are vulnerable to developing an addiction and that all it takes is for a confluence of factors to make someone an addict. I have seen extremely strong and resilient individuals develop addictions just because their pain was just too overwhelming.

Indeed, it is often about uncovering the psychological pain that helps explain why someone develops an addiction. Many people who have an addiction often have deep rooted causes of pain. This could be pain from having a traumatic childhood or from adverse experiences later in life. Such pain lends a hand in these challenging circumstances to a person using alcohol or substances as a means to cope with the pain. A story of pain or trauma often belies any addiction and Dr Gabor Mate has expounded this best when he says, "The question is not why the addiction, but why the pain."

When people use substances or alcohol to cope with pain, it is not "being weak". Very often, from an outsider's point of view, it is easy to judge someone for having an addiction, as being weak, as taking the "easy" way out to cope with pain. This narrative is untrue and unhelpful, to say the least. It misses out on the fundamental principle that no one chooses to be an addict, much less being able to choose our life circumstances.

However, it is also important to acknowledge that the initial decision to use drugs or substances is something that people have control over, insofar as the decision-making capacity has not yet been compromised as addiction has not yet set in. This is needed for public education efforts and its important especially where our youth is concerned. That initial decision to use any drugs or alcohol can be a slippery slope towards developing a lifelong addiction.

In my talks to various health professionals, I always stress the point that once an addiction is formed, the remission rates are not good as addiction is often an intractable illness. There can be periods of remission interspersed with periods of relapses. Hence the best way of tackling an addiction is really to prevent it from being formed in the first place.

That being said, I also firmly believe that many times we also do not have much control over our life circumstances and there may often be times when the pain is just too much to bear and the person then uses substances or alcohol as a means to cope.

Without any other support mechanisms, this way of coping then becomes the path of least resistance. Done often enough, an addiction then forms, and the brain's reward mechanisms gets hijacked, leading to a repeated pattern of behaviours once the addiction is set in motion. This firing of the reward pathway then re-kindles repeatedly once the person is exposed to the right set of cues or triggers.

How to be Kind to Others

This section deals with how to interact with someone with an addiction, how to speak without triggering him or her and how to be compassionate above all else. It also provides tips on how to give the right nudges to people to motivate them into action.

Motivational Interviewing

Motivational Interviewing was developed by William R. Miller and Stephen Rollnick[1] as a counselling approach based on the client centred humanistic approach of Carl Rogers. Although it has often been cited as helping people with addiction issues change their behaviour through certain skills such as empathy and providing unconditional positive regard, it is also helpful as a means to nudge any kind of behaviour change.

As can be seen in the figure below, which depicts the transtheoretical model[2] or more commonly known as the stages of change model, a person goes through various "mental stages" in his change journey. There are a few stages in this model, from pre-contemplation to contemplation and then to preparation, action and maintenance. Relapse is featured in the centre of this model as a person theoretically can relapse at any stage of the journey.

The different stages are defined as such:

Pre-contemplation: Not considering change
Contemplation: Considering change, ambivalent
Preparation: Committed to change
Action: Change behaviour has started
Maintenance: Change of behaviour is well established

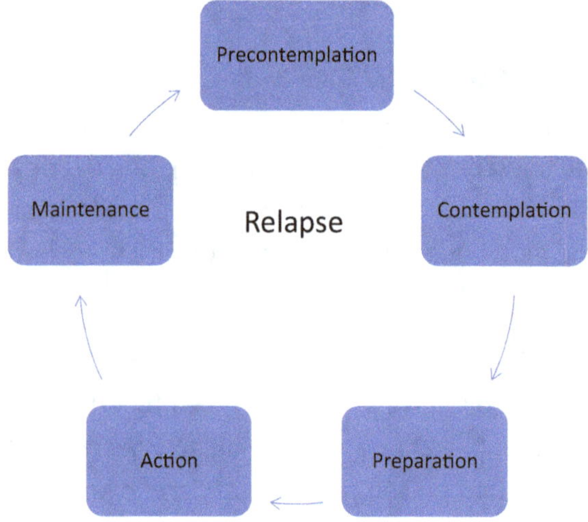

Figure: Transtheoretical model for change.

The importance of knowing this model of change is so that we can apply the right techniques when interacting with people about their addiction. When a person is in the pre-contemplative stage of change, they are not considering change of their behaviour. At this stage, generally motivational interviewing is not going to work as the person is not ready to make a change and generally, just providing some advice or information regarding their illness and directing them to the appropriate resources when they are ready would be the way forwards.

Many well-intentioned relatives or friends would bring the person or literally "drag" them to the clinic for treatment at this stage thinking that the problem would be solved once the person is in the clinic. However, if the person is pre-contemplative about change, this can be detrimental to the relationship with the person and can be seen as intrusive and unhelpful, further worsening the therapeutic outcome. Indeed, we can sometimes do too much at this stage by nagging or forcibly trying to engage the patient in treatment when he or she is not ready, thereby trying to do the right thing and yet being "unkind".

Once a person is in the contemplative stage of change when he or she is considering change, we are then able to use the tools of motivational interviewing to engage the patient in the change journey, eliciting what is known as "change talk" as opposed to "sustain talk" with regards to the patient's current behaviour that we are attempting to change.

This process utilizes the patient's own resources and "rolls with the patient's resistance" to change and is skilfully done to ensure the person is in control of his or her own motivations. Very frequently change is not so easy and just telling a person to change his or her behaviour would frequently encounter resistance from the person. Hence motivational interviewing does not directly confront the person with regards to his or her own behaviour but gently explores the impact of a particular behaviour on the person's life and what he or she feels or is ready to do about it. An example of such a dialogue will be illustrated below.

Thereafter once a person is in the action stages of change, motivational interviewing or enhancement techniques can be utilized further to anchor the change progress that has been made and help prevent relapses. Usually, motivational interviewing techniques are paired with cognitive behaviour principles once the person has reached the action and maintenance stages of change.

An example of a motivational interviewing dialogue

Therapist: How has your alcohol use affected your life. Tell me some of the good things that alcohol has done for you and some of the not so good things?

Patient: Alcohol use has helped me cope with my job demands and really has been an aid when I am severely stressed. However, sometimes I get intoxicated and end up getting a hangover which makes me unable to work the next day. My bosses have commented that my absenteeism rate is high.

Therapist: It seems that you really value your work quite a lot but at the same time, it is causing you a lot of stress. You feel that alcohol helps you cope but also affects your work negatively. If that's how you feel, is there perhaps a need to moderate how much you are drinking?

Patient: Yes, I have been trying to but sometimes I can get too caught up in everything and I cannot seem to control my drinking once I have started, and then it ends up in a vicious cycle of me being intoxicated.

Therapist: It's good that you have been working on controlling how much you are drinking, even though it doesn't seem to have worked as you wanted it to. Perhaps then, rather than stop trying, we need to analyze what has worked for you in the past and what hasn't?

Patient: Yes, I think that would be helpful. What do you suggest?

The above example is just one way a therapist might use motivational interviewing strategies to help a patient manage his or her alcohol use. The patient is prone to binge drinking and seems unable to stop once he or she starts drinking. The therapist acknowledges that the patient is aware of the problem and has made efforts to control the issue whilst at the same time exploring the motivations for the patient to continue drinking.

This is done in a non-confrontational manner and allows the patient to explore his or her motivations to want to quit drinking. Notice that no solutions have been offered to the patient as motivational interviewing is about helping the person find his or her own solutions and utilize his internal and external resources to help solve the issue at hand. This is the client centred approach that is also known as the Rogerian approach that is kind to the person and also facilitates change best.

Motivational Interviewing is one of the best ways to help someone with an addiction and it is really a way of communication. A simple way of remembering how to do motivational interviewing is using the FRAMES model, where F stands for feedback, R for responsibility, A for advice, M for Menu of Options, E for Empathy and S for self-efficacy.[3]

During the counselling process, providing regular **feedback**, about discrepancies between the person's current actions and his or her own intended goals is one of the aims of motivational interviewing at encouraging behaviour change. In terms of responsibility, it is highlighted to the person that the **responsibility** of changing the behaviour in question belongs to him or her and that the counsellor's role is to facilitate this change journey. In terms of **advice**, this advice should be given in delicate manner, with the patient's goal and decision in mind and not offering unsolicited advice. Rather, working with the patient so as to provide the advice when requested is important. **Menu** of options means providing the person with a range of choices in which he or she is able to enact the behaviour change and so encourages flexibility and control over the process. **Empathy** implies being understanding and appreciative that change is a difficult process and this can be shown through various techniques of conversation that will be covered later. **Self-efficacy** means reaffirming the person that he or she has the resources for change and supporting his or her own journey in achieving this.

Techniques of Conversation that Promote Empathy

There are several techniques that can be utilized in conversation with someone who has an addiction in order to facilitate understanding and sharing, thereby creating empathy and a psychological safe space for further sharing. These techniques will be covered here.

Ask Open-ended Questions

Open-ended questions are the opposite to close-ended questions which encourage elaboration on a topic instead of just providing yes-no answers. This style of questioning is generally seen as less intrusive and encourages dialogue.

Examples of open-ended questions are as follows:

1. How was your day today?
2. What is going through your mind now?
3. Where do you see yourself now in terms of your recovery journey?
4. When is an appropriate time for us to talk more?
5. Why has the situation gotten so bad this time?

As can be seen from the above examples, open-ended questions tend to involve the 4Ws (What, Where, When, Why) and 1H (How)? These types of questions can be used to open up a dialogue and are seen as less interrogative. Asking "how was your day today?", instead of saying, "Are you feeling all right?" is much better at eliciting a response from someone. Saying "Are you feeling all right?" is more of yes-no type of close-ended question and doesn't really help to elicit more conversation. At the start of any conversation, generally open ended questions set the stage for how the rest of the conversation or dialogue will proceed and asking the right open ended questions will go a long way towards facilitating any dialogue.

Clarifying

Clarifying is another useful technique that should be applied to enhance the building of empathy in a dialogue with someone who may be suffering from an addiction. This helps because we don't assume something that is unclear and instead seek to enhance our understanding of the other person's experience. An example is given below.

John: I am feeling extremely tired today. Everybody has been giving me a hard time. I am not sure what is wrong with me as well. Everything seems to be going wrong today.

Family member: It seems like you are having a very difficult time today and I would like to find out more about what's been happening that is causing you distress. Would you be able to tell me more about your day?

This act of clarifying then helps the person open up further and takes away any underlying assumption of what is going on. Sometimes, assuming that a person's bad day is due to something can set you off on the wrong footing, especially if the assumption is wrong and based on underlying prejudices. So at all times, it is better to clarify if you are unsure.

Paraphrasing and Summarizing

Paraphrasing and summarizing are useful tools to signal understanding to the client or interviewee. It also promotes empathy by allowing the interviewer to process what the interviewee has said and then rephrase in his or her own words in a succinct manner. An example is given below.

Jane: There is a lot of stress going on in my workplace. Colleagues are not friendly to me and pushing work to me. My boss is scolding me as I am unable to meet timelines for projects.

My whole life is in a mess and my husband is not at home, always out drinking late with his friends. Can you blame me for drinking alcohol to cope. Why does my husband get to have all the fun. Does anyone ever blame him for drinking instead of me? Why do I always have to stay at home to look after the children?

Family member: You feel as if your life is spiralling out of control with difficulties at work and with not much support from your husband. Drinking alcohol is your way of coping with the stress of work and looking after children. It appears that you may need some help in this regard.

Notice that paraphrasing the person's problems in your own words and then summarizing her difficulties has a powerful effect at demonstrating empathy by showing to the person that we are listening actively to him or her. This then helps us connect to the person or family member better.

Reflective Listening

Reflective listening is a skill in which we can use to reflect back the words but more importantly, the emotions to the person after we have heard the contents of their conversation. This shows that we have been paying attention to the individual and is an important skill of active listening. An example is given below.

James: I am sick and tired of being told constantly what to do, how to behave or that I need to change my drug use habits. I am in a lot of pain, and you don't know what I have been going through. I think you would be coping much worse than me if you were in my shoes.

Family member: I am sorry that you are going through so much currently and I wish that things could have been better for you. It seems that you are not coping well with the pain and had to rely on certain drugs to manage the pain. This must indeed not be easy considering how the drugs you are using are also affecting your health. Could I speak to you more about what is causing this pain as I wish to understand your situation a bit better.

In the above example, James has expressed that he is going through a lot of pain, and he has alluded to using drugs to cope with this pain. He is also tired of being judged for his drug use habits. What the family member has done through reflective listening is to pick up on this pain and how James is not coping well with it. The family member also highlighted that he or she would like to know more about the causes of this pain so as to open up the conversation further whilst at the same time expressing empathy for James' condition. Notice that the family member has also skilfully "seeded" in the information that drug use is detrimental to James' health and in so doing, possibly encouraged James to think about his drug use habits without directly confronting him about this.

Mirroring

Mirroring is a particular useful technique to engage a person in dialogue. This is done through "copycat" mechanisms. For instance, if a person is feeling sad and speaking in a slow manner. Then the interviewer or the family member then mirrors this pace of speaking. If a person sits back in a relaxed and open posture, then the interviewer also sits back in a relaxed and open posture. This mirroring of the speech and the posture helps to create a sense of commonness or likeness to the individual and helps the person to relate better to you subconsciously.

Hopefully, the above techniques can be applied to help you better engage a patient who is suffering from an addiction.

References

1. Miller WR, Rollnick S. Motivational interviewing: preparing people to change addictive behaviour. New York Guilford Press, 1991:30–5
2. Prochaska JO, Velicer WF. The transtheoretical model of health behavior change. Am J Health Promot. 1997 Sep-Oct;12(1):38–48.
3. Miller, W. R., & Sanchez, V. C. (1994). Motivating young adults for treatment and lifestyle change. In G. S. Howard & P. E. Nathan (Eds.), Alcohol use and misuse by young adults (pp. 55–81). University of Notre Dame Press.

QUIZ TIME 8:

1. What is motivational interviewing?

    a) An interrogative technique

    b) A conversational technique to encourage
        behaviour change

    c) A way of calming a person down

    d) A method of eliciting information

2. What is mirroring?

    a) A technique to create a sense of commonness
        with the interviewee.

    b) Looking into the mirror to practice going through
        an interview

    c) Looking at an ongoing interview with the help of
        a one-way mirror

    d) A type of covert recording during an interview

3. Which of the following stages of change is motivational interviewing generally not applied?

    a) Contemplative

    b) Preparation

    c) Action

    d) Pre-contemplative

9

WE ARE ALL IN THIS TOGETHER

This next chapter is dedicated to providing a snapshot of how various agencies work together in concert to provide treatment for patients with addiction. Not all patients with addiction need to come to specialist treatment services. Many patients also seek help with faith-based services and primary care providers when they develop an addiction.

What a specialist treatment service provides is access to medications and a multi-disciplinary team to provide tertiary level care for patients who need more intensive treatment. For example, at the National Addictions Management Service (NAMS), we offer both inpatient and outpatient treatments for difficult to manage addictions. The inpatient treatment programme consists of a detoxification phase which typically is for one week in duration and a rehabilitation phase which is for another 3 weeks. The purpose of the inpatient detoxification programme is for close supervised monitoring during the time when a person is expected to undergo withdrawal from the substances he or she is taking. During this period of supervised monitoring, the patient will also be given medications to help ameliorate the withdrawal symptoms. This will make the process of undergoing withdrawal easier as opposed to undergoing detoxification "cold turkey".

After the person has "detoxed" from the substance, then the person would undergo the next phase of the inpatient programme. This is the rehabilitation programme whereby the psychosocial aspects of addiction treatment would come in. This generally involves attending individual and group counselling sessions as well as taking part in various occupational therapy activities. Family sessions would also be conducted as well to brief and educate the family members about addictions. During this time, the patient will also be given information about the various community supports that are available and to seek help thereafter at some of these agencies if required. Some of our patients will also be referred to various Social Service Agencies (SSAs) for various forms of help pertaining to their Addictions after being discharged. Other patients may benefit from an extended period of stay at a residential treatment programme provided for at a Halfway House for continued psychosocial rehabilitation.

Besides NAMS, as mentioned, many other providers feature in helping patients with addictions. Many of them are SSAs and some prominent examples here are We Care, SANA and NCADA. Many of the SSAs provide counselling services and some also provide these services for the patient's families as well. What is helpful is that some SSAs such as One Hope also provide counselling services for behavioural addictions such as Gambling Disorder and these services are provided at no cost to the client. Indeed, the network of counselling centres out there including counselling services being provided in schools, Halfway houses, prisons and other faith-based groups are all important in providing a web of support for those afflicted with addictions.

Peer Support

One important element in recovery is peer support and for this it is important to mention groups such as Narcotics Anonymous (NA), Alcoholics Anonymous (AA), Gamblers Anonymous (GA) and Sex and Love Addicts Anonymous (SLAA). Such groups provide the support of peers in recovery. Peers are persons with lived-in experience for the illness in question (e.g. alcohol dependence or drug dependence) and these groups sessions provide them an opportunity to meet up regularly to get support from each other. These facilitated sessions encourage sharing by other Peers and allow those afflicted with the addiction to get help, support and validation from others going through the same illness. Very often, during these sessions, one also gets connected with Sponsors who are big brothers or sisters that can provide emergency help when required, who are just a phone call way.

The value in such group-based support services led by peers makes sense for addictions as it is very difficult for the laymen and even professional counsellors to be able to understand fully what some of these patients are going through. Also, the power of anecdotes and the ability to tell stories of recovery from the standpoint of a person who has gone through it before is much more powerful and influential on another recovering person than something perhaps a health professional would be able to say.

Of course, groups may not be helpful for everyone, and it is important whilst attending groups to take part actively so as to obtain the full beneficial experience of such group support. Groups like NA and AA are based on the 12-Step approach and one of these steps is surrendering to a higher power and hence people who cannot accept this will have difficulty fitting in. Also, people who have difficulty sharing in groups, or have interpersonal difficulties or who are introverted may also not benefit as much from such group support.

Whilst peer support is indeed very important and beneficial to the recovering addict, very often, the first point of help or support to him or her would come from the family.

What can a family member do to help someone struggling with an addiction? Very often such individuals are heavily engaged with their addiction and have no insight into their illness, shunning family members and even treatment agencies. How do you help someone who doesn't want to be helped?

At this juncture, it is important to bring back the Transtheoretical model or commonly known as the stages of change model.[1]

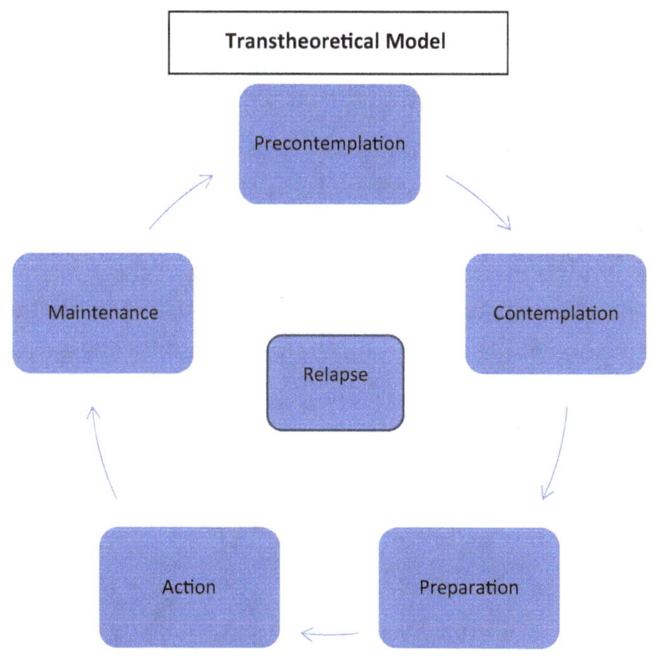

Transtheoretical Model

This is a very dynamic model even though the arrows are depicted moving from pre-contemplation to contemplation and then to preparation, action, and maintenance. The dynamicity of this model means that a person can move between different stages fairly rapidly and sometimes appear to bypass certain stages. An example being a person going from contemplation

stage of change to the action stage of change without having gone through the preparation stage. Another person could be in the preparation stage of change, then suddenly relapse into drug using behaviour. Such is the nature of addictions and the unpredictability of it, that relapse can happen at any time. Hence relapse is put at the centre of this model, to remind us that it can happen at any stage of the illness.

What is very helpful though is that this model allows us to conceptualize what type of interventions to provide at each stage of a patient's journey. We have asked the question earlier of what family members can do in the event that patients themselves are unwilling to share or engage in treatment for their addictions. Such patients are frequently in the pre-contemplative stage of change. At this point in time, the patients are not considering change and any form of counselling is usually not going to be helpful.

Generally, even if patients are brought by family members to attend sessions at NAMS during this stage of the illness, counselling by our NAMS counsellors are unlikely to be helpful and what we often provide at this stage of the illness is psychoeducation about the harms of drug use and providing knowledge about the resources available in the community should the patients wish to seek

help. We also educate family members about how to interact with the patient to provide the necessary support without being too critical of his or her addiction. Lastly, we also provide supportive counselling to the caregiver or family member as it is understandably a time of great distress to the family as a whole. This is an important element of the treatment plan as without healing the family as a unit, sometimes it is very hard for the treatment of the individual concerned to proceed far.

When the person afflicted with the addiction is considering change of his or her behaviour and has gone on to the contemplation stage of change, this is when techniques of motivational interviewing can be brought in to facilitate change in a person's behaviour. This is also the time when the family member can provide the necessary supportive counselling to the afflicted person as they may be more receptive of the advice given or be brought in for treatment. Once a person has managed to engage in treatment either in the preparation, action or maintenance stages of change, the role of the family becomes even more important to walk with them in their change journey. It is important for the family to understand that slips or relapses are common in this journey of change and not to berate the individual for falling in the event of a slip or relapse. The family members can help to identify slips early and nudge the patient back into treatment when it happens. They can also provide a supportive and conducive environment at home for recovery to take place.

Of course, it's not always easy for family members to shoulder the whole responsibility of looking after a patient afflicted with addictions, especially when the family environment sometimes is the source of the stress and instability in a person's life. For such instances and for protracted periods of rehabilitation, there are residential programmes provided at various halfway houses to help an individual in his or her recovery journey. Such residential halfway houses integrate counselling, work, psychoeducation groups, spirituality, journalling, and various other modalities into a person's residential stay to incorporate some element of structure and routine into the individual's life. Over time, then a person gains mastery and skills to be able to transit to independent living on his or her own.

Upstream Work

Besides the role of family members, various treatment agencies and halfway house residential programmes, there is also much important educational work that is done by various agencies such as the Central Narcotics Bureau, Ministry of Education and the Health Promotion Board. Such agencies provide preventative education towards the harms of drug use (CNB, MOE) as well as alcohol use, vaping and smoking (MOE, HPB) so as to be able to prevent addiction from forming in the first place. There are also other agencies such as the National Council on Problem Gambling (NCPG) which creates awareness and provides much needed education on the harms of problem gambling.

Upstream education is important as it helps to prevent an addiction from forming in the first place. Various social service agencies such as IMPART as well as the Singapore Youth Council also help empower our Youth to be more resilient and form communities to support Youth. The truth is that having such community networks is important as "connection" to such support networks is often the way to beat an addiction, by fostering a sense of belonging and being integrated into the community at large instead of relying on just oneself to face struggles alone.

Often, I see families being fragmented because of drug use. Some teens I see come from families where their parents have used drugs or alcohol, and some have parents who are in and out of prison. For these children who have been exposed to the harms of drug use at such a young age, often various agencies such as the prison services, ministry of home affairs, social service agencies and religious groups have come into their lives early to provide the necessary support.

Without such community level involvement, medical care alone is unable to ameliorate the conditions of the family much and prevent the trajectory of the next generation away from drug use. Hence for these families, such upstream work is even more important for the next generation to provide a more stable home environment and linkage to community resources, to prevent the same cycle of drug and alcohol use from ensuing.

Interweaving

A whole of society's effort is needed when we talk about addiction management, from prevention to treatment. This involves a concerted effort by different ministries and also ground up movements to support those afflicted with addictions. Various ministries such as the Ministry of Health, Ministry of Home Affairs, Ministry of Social and Family Services and Ministry of Education have chipped in to manage this problem and we can take heart that you are truly not alone in facing an addiction. The key is to access the services early and have the knowledge of which services to access. Community support structures are there to ensure that help is readily available, even though sometimes the stigma prevents the user from seeking help. Hence, we must all chip in to encourage people we know who have an addiction to seek help early.

Tiered Model of Care

Singapore has a National Mental Health and Well-being Strategy that aims to make mental healthcare accessible and effective in addressing the needs of the population. This divides the mental health requirements of the population into 4 tiers to cater to the differing levels of needs.[2]

Tier 1 refers to Mental Well-being promotion and the aim is to promote mental wellness for the population and prevent the onset of mental illnesses. This would therefore involve education in schools as well as public education to raise awareness and help the people develop resilience.

Tier 2 refers to the provision of Low intensity services for those with mild symptoms such as those with mild stress or anxiety or mood symptoms to prevent worsening of these symptoms. Such Tier 2 level of care can be provided by various mental health professionals, such as social workers and counsellors working in the community.

Tier 3 refers to the provision of Moderate intensity services for those with moderate symptoms of mental illness and these usually involve more specialized care with inputs from psychologists or medical professionals.

Tier 4 refers to the provision of High intensity services for those with complex mental health needs and this might involve multidisciplinary team inputs and specialist care and possibly even inpatient admissions.

This tiered system of care also applies to the management of addictions in Singapore. Many times, important Tier 1 work and public education efforts on drugs are done by agencies such as the ministry of education in schools as well as enforcement agencies such as the Central Narcotics Bureau. Our Health Promotion Board does important tier 1 work pertaining to smoking, vaping and alcohol.

Tier 2 work pertaining to addictions is done by mental health professionals from various counselling centres, family service centres, faith-based groups such as mosques, churches etc.

Tier 3 work pertaining to addictions is managed by various Social Service Agencies such as SANA, We Care, primary care general practitioners, doctors working at restructured hospitals and also the team working at the National Addictions Management Service

Tier 4 work pertaining to addictions is managed mainly by the National Addictions Management Service as this needs specialized multidisciplinary team inputs as well as by teams providing residential rehabilitation at the Halfway Houses.

List of Resources for the Tiered Model of Care in Addictions (Non-exhaustive)

Tier 1 (Health Promotion, Public Education)	HPB (alcohol, smoking vaping) Ministry of Education National Council Against Drug Abuse Central Narcotics Bureau National Council on Problem Gambling (Gambling)
Tier 2 (Low intensity services for those mildy affected)	Faith-based counselling services Family service centres School Counsellors

Tier 3 (Moderate Intensity Services)	One Hope Centre (Behavioural Addictions) Singapore Anti-Narcotics Association Primary Care Network (Smoking, Alcohol, Vaping) Restructured Hospitals, private hospitals We Care Community Services Limited National Addictions Management Service
Tier 4 (High intensity services for complex needs)	National Addictions Management Service (inpatient and outpatient services) Halfway Houses (residential rehabilitation)

References

1. Prochaska JO, Velicer WF. The transtheoretical model of health behavior change. Am J Health Promot. 1997 Sep-Oct;12(1):38–48.
2. National Mental Health and Well-being Strategy (2023) | Ministry of Health

QUIZ TIME 9:

1. What is an example of Tier 4 care for addictions?

    a) Inpatient admission for complex addictions management

    b) Addictions education in schools

    c) Addictions management at primary care settings

    d) Addictions management at a counselling centre

2. Which of the following is not a social service agency managing addictions?

    a) SANA

    b) We Care

    c) One Hope

    d) NAMS

3. Which ministries/agencies are not involved in the
   work against addictions?

   a) MSF

   b) MHA

   c) MOH

   d) NEA

10

LEGAL ASPECTS & THE ADDICTION EQUATION RE-VISITED

This is perhaps one of the most difficult chapters for me to write as I am primarily a psychiatrist whose main interest is in addictions, rather than forensics.

As we are aware, Singapore has very tough drug laws and there is also the death penalty in Singapore which largely is there to deter traffickers. There is also the misuse of drugs regulation-19 (MDR-19) which stipulates that medical practitioners have a duty to report patients suspected to be drug addicts to the Director of the Central Narcotics Bureau. Singapore classifies drugs into 3 classes (A, B and C) with the highest penalties meted out to people who are found to be in possession of class A drugs (see table below). Once you exceed a certain amount in your possession, the onus then falls on the individual to prove that he or she wasn't trafficking the drugs.

With such tough drug laws in Singapore and our zero-tolerance policy towards drugs, how then do addiction psychiatrists practice and what is our role towards helping those afflicted addictions? Not an easy question to answer indeed.

There are many instances in my line of work where the intersection of addiction and the law occur, one of which is the mandatory reporting requirement mentioned earlier in the MDR-19. The other aspect is when I am being asked to do forensic assessments for patients who have been charged with offences involving drug consumption, possession and even trafficking. Some of these assessments involve patients who have committed offences whilst under the influence of substances or alcohol and some have even committed offences to finance their addictions.

However, for the vast majority of times, the patients I had seen have not been involved with the criminal justice system for their addictions, especially when we talk about legal substances like alcohol, or other legal forms of activity such as gambling, gaming etc. Those patients who see me for drug use were mainly involved with the criminal justice system as they had gone through drug rehabilitation programmes in the Drug rehabilitation centres (DRC). In fact, the DSM-IV had particularly taken out the criteria on criminal involvement when it consolidated the abuse and dependence criteria in the DSM-5 revision on alcohol and substance use disorders.

Very often, my patients will ask if they will be arrested if they seek treatment with us, since their details would be reported to the authorities. As such, many patients understandably would feel reluctant to come forth and seek treatment. There is no easy answer to this, and the truth is, my role is here to help patients as best as I can whilst following the mandatory requirements put forth by the law. However, I am also aware that the law is in place for a reason, and we try to work within the confines of the law to help our patients, many of whom still continue to seek treatment with us.

Classes of Drugs	Examples
A	Amphetamine, Cannabis, Buprenorphine, Diamorphine, morphine, Cocaine
B	Codeine, Dihydrocodeine, Methylphenidate
C	Nimetazepam, Flunitrazepam, Mephentermine

Does Addiction Cause a Person to Commit Crimes?

I have written many forensic reports in my training as a psychiatrist and have been to courts to defend my opinions on several occasions. This is not something that I enjoy. Very often, I am called upon as an expert witness and have to provide a psychiatric opinion on a case to see if there is any causal or contributory link between the accused's mental health condition and the offence/s that he or she has committed.

McNaughton's Rules

To qualify for a defence of insanity or unsoundness of mind, the defendant needs to prove that he was labouring from a disease of the mind such that he was unable to appreciate the nature of his act or if he did, he did not know that what he did was wrong.

It's usually applied to Major Mental Health conditions where the suffer was labouring under hallucinations or delusions such that they have an impaired reality testing, not being to differentiate what is real from what is not real.

From an addiction point of view, sometimes what is asked is if the defendant was of unsound mind if the offence was committed when the person was intoxicated.

This is clearly a tricky proposition as if a person can be stated to be of unsound mind when intoxicated, then the person can technically not be responsible for any of the crimes he or she has committed whilst labouring under the effects of substances. This inherently does not make much sense as if a person has knowingly gotten intoxicated despite knowing that he or she would be in such a state for example after a few drinks, then he or she should still be held responsible for getting themselves into such a state.

An example of such a scenario is when a person has committed an aggressive act or assaulted someone after being intoxicated with alcohol. The defendant claims that he wasn't aware of the entire episode of assaulting a stranger he met in the pub as he was intoxicated. He cannot remember events leading up to the act and cannot remember having attacked the victim despite being shown videos of the incriminating act. He is otherwise a regular drinker and is aware of the limits of his drinking before which he would become intoxicated. He has even gotten into episodes of altercation with others previously after being intoxicated despite not being charged for those episodes. The lawyer representing him claims that he does not have the requisite "mens rea" or "guilty mind" that is necessary to commit the offence as he is not able to form the intention to hurt anyone in his incapacitated state of mind after being intoxicated.

Is such a defence therefore reasonable? The short answer is that the defendant is a chronic drinker who has knowingly gotten himself into such a state based on his past history of being intoxicated and therefore should not be absolved from voluntarily getting himself into such a state of affairs. Again, this is for the courts to decide but the opinion of the expert witness psychiatrist probably would not deviate too much from this assessment.

You may ask what happens then if it's the first time that the person has gotten intoxicated and has never been in such a situation before? What then would the expert opinion of the psychiatrist be? Voluntary intoxication even if it's the first time that a person has gotten intoxicated will generally not be mitigating if the person has knowingly consumed something that is an intoxicant. Also claiming that he or she did not know the substance consumed was an intoxicant would depend on whether a reasonable person objectively should know or understand that the substance consumed would likely cause some level of intoxication. Of course, it would also depend on the specifics of the case at hand but generally speaking, such defence is hard to get by.

Contributory Link to Offences

There have been some instances where despite not being causal to the defendant committing an offence, there may be some psychiatric conditions that may contribute to a person committing an offence.

One of the natural things that comes to mind for some people is that one of the hallmark features of an addiction is this inability or lack of control pertaining to their behaviours in question. If so, this might lead one to ask questions such as if a person has a gambling disorder, then does this addiction lead the person to have lack of control over what he does to finance his addiction? There have been some people who have embezzled money or even resorted to cheating or stealing to finance their gambling addiction. Wouldn't the very nature of them suffering an addiction contribute to their offences, if the money that was illegally obtained was meant to finance their addiction? Another example could be a person with an alcohol use disorder arguing that him stealing alcohol from a convenience store was because he has an intractable urge or craving for alcohol and couldn't control his behaviour.

Such arguments are tenuous at best and when accepted lead to a slippery slope in terms of what can be considered contributory in nature.

Many times, even though the addiction is very severe in nature, if you ask the person if he or she is aware for example about the unlawful nature of an act, e.g. such as stealing money or stealing alcohol, they would be able to appreciate that what they were doing were wrong and it was a conscious choice to still pursue what they were doing. They would have a range of options to manage their condition and this would include borrowing money from friends or relatives which they might have tried before which are not illegal. Hence the decision to commit an offence can only really be considered to have been contributed by their addiction if there was really a strong association between what they are suffering from and the offence itself. This has to be tried in court and accepted by the Judge.

Revisiting the Addiction Equation

After reading so much about addiction and being introduced to the Addiction equation in chapter 1, it's my hope that your understanding and appreciation of Addiction has changed.

Let's revisit the addiction equation.

$$\text{Severity of Addiction} = \frac{(\text{Pleasure} + \text{Urge}) \times \text{Speed}^2}{\text{Control}}$$

 CHAPTER 10

Pleasure-Degree of positive sensations derived
Speed-Frequency of onset of a particular behaviour
Urge-The desire to use a particular substance or perform a behaviour
Control-Ability to exercise judgement and restraint in carrying out a particular behaviour

Pleasure: 1–5, where 1 is almost no pleasure, 2 is little pleasure, 3 is moderate pleasure, 4 is significantly high pleasure and 5 is very high pleasure, measured in terms of the degree or magnitude of positive sensations derived from an activity.

Urge: 1–5, where 1 is almost no urge, 2 is little urge, 3 is moderate degree of urge, 4 is significant urge and 5 is very high degree of urge, measured in terms of the desire to use a substance or perform a particular activity.

Speed: 1–5, where 1 is activity that takes place very slowly, 2 where activity is slow, 3 where activity is moderate in speed, 4 where activity is fast and 5 where the activity takes place very rapidly.

Control: 1–5, where 1 is almost no control, 2 is little control, 3 is moderate degree of control, 4 is a lot of control and 5 is absolute control over a particular activity.

In terms of the equation, the maximum score that can be derived is

$$(5 + 5) \times 5^2/1 = 250$$

The minimum score that can be derived is

$$(1 + 1) \times 1^2/5 = 2/5$$

So the range is from 2/5 to 250, when we quantify the severity of an addiction.

We have also defined low severity as 2/5 to 25, moderate severity as 26 to 100 and high severity as 101–250.

Jus to reiterate here that this equation is really about determining the severity of an addiction based on the variables mentioned here. It is not meant for use in diagnosing if someone has an addiction. For that purpose, there are diagnostic criteria mentioned in the DSM-5 or ICD-11 that are used.

The importance of this equation then lies in

1. Determining how severe an addiction problem is
2. Prognosticating
3. Highlighting which variables are most affected by the addiction and then subsequently determining treatment plans

The ways to manage an addiction based on these variables have been explored in depth in chapter 7. However, we also know that as addiction is a chronic disease influenced by many social determinants of health; addressing the medical aspects alone are not going to be extremely effective. Hence, in chapter 9, we looked at the role of various organizations in providing both upstream preventive work as well as downstream rehabilitative work.

For any equation to work, it must consider the real world we are currently living in. Certainly, an equation like this necessarily invokes much debate as to the necessity of having it since the conceptualization of any psychiatric ailments already involve well established frameworks such as the biopsychosocial model established by George Engel in 1977. This equation then value adds by helping us distil down to the very variables that I believe are quintessential to all types of addiction.

As mentioned, having a knowledge of how severe a patient's addiction is on a scale of 2/5 to 250 and what variables are most affected allows us to consider what needs to be done to address the addiction most. For instance, if urge is deemed to be the main contributor to the person's severity of addiction, then intervention needs to adequately address this component. Or if control or the lack thereof is found to be the main contributor for a person's addiction, then treatment must necessarily involve ways to help the patient gain mastery or control of his behaviour. In the latter instance, targeting pleasure or urge or speed would then be the wrong focus.

This is the first time to my knowledge that an equation has been conceptualized to measure the severity of addictive disorders and it is conceivable that there may be better versions in future that better accounts for the complexity of this problem. Again, whether it is used subsequently in clinical practice or whether it is practical to do so remains to be seen.

The aim of this book then is not so much about this equation as to provide awareness of what addictions is about and I hope the various chapters has done this topic justice, especially to people who have no prior knowledge whatsoever about addictions. Indeed, the equation is mainly to spark interest in a subject matter that is not often talked about and that continues to attract much stigma in today's society.

As we have discussed in chapter 9, many of the interventions require a whole of society effort to help the patient and their families. Having an addiction is not just a medical problem but also a societal problem at large, requiring interweaving of services to be able to address this properly.

Despite the prognosis of addictive disorders not being so good in terms of remission rates, there are effective interventions, and the outcomes can be significantly improved if the condition is detected early. Patients must also be aware of the services that are available for them to seek help with, and it is with this intention that we have elaborated on this in chapter 9.

The field of addictions is also constantly evolving, especially in the realm of digital addictions. It is for this reason that there was a separate chapter on this in chapter 5.

Application Exercises

After having covered the addiction equation, let's have a few application exercises to see the utility of this equation.

Case scenario 1:

Mr. Lim is a 40 year old male who is currently at the emergency department of a restructured hospital and he is experiencing severe withdrawals from alcohol, having very bad shakes and anxiety. He drinks one litre of vodka every day from 9 am in the morning to 11pm at night and he spaces his intake every 15 minutes of so with a few sips each time. He says he does so in order to avoid severe tremors. Currently, he reports that he last drank alcohol two hours ago and is having severe cravings. He has 1 year history of heavy regular drinking and he mentioned that he started drinking heavily after he had lost his job one year ago. The longest he can stop drinking for is only for several hours before he gets uncontrollable shakes and anxiety. His mood has not been very good for the past one year as well, having passive suicidal thoughts as well due to his poor socioeconomic situation after losing his job. He mentions that alcohol does provide him some relieve over his low moods and he feels better after drinking, albeit only for a short while and he feels worse soon after. This has caused a vicious cycle of drinking and now he is unable to stop. He feels that he has totally lost control over his drinking and is aware that it's causing him multiple health problems as well as relationship problems with his spouse. He hopes to be admitted for detoxification from alcohol as he has had seizures after stopping drinking and is worried about having seizures again. What is the severity of his alcohol dependence?

For Mr Lim's scenario, let's first quantify the variables in the addiction equation.

For this case, I would define pleasure as 2, urge as 5, speed as 5 and control as 1

In terms of the severity, it would therefore be

$$(2 + 5) \times 5^2/1 = 175$$

This would definitely signify a high severity of addiction.

Let's explain why I have quantified the variables in this manner. I have defined pleasure as 2 in this example as Mr. Lim does still derive pleasure from his drinking and it does help to relieve his negative moods to a certain extent. However, the

pleasure is not significant as he feels worse soon after. In terms of urge, there are strong cravings to drink and he needs to drink every 15 minutes or so in order to avoid tremors or withdrawal symptoms. This signifies very strong urges, hence urge has been quantified as 5. Next, I have quantified speed as 5 as well. The reason for this is that Mr. Lim is drinking alcohol every 15 minutes or so and this is an extremely high rate of reinforcement especially when we take into consideration the activity. Of course, one may say that compared to the speed of using social media or gaming, drinking every few minutes does not seem so high. However, the speed quantification has to be dependent on the type of activity and hence it's not possible to compare across addictions and has to be referenced to that particular activity in question. So 15 minutes intervals when it pertains to alcohol use can be considered very fast. Lastly, control is noticeably absent as well and Mr. Lim has not managed to control his drinking to the extent that he is unable to stop drinking and manages to do so only for several hours at most, hence I've indicated control as 1.

Now let's look at further examples.

Scenario 2

Susan is a 50-year-old lady who is currently seeing you in the outpatient clinic. She reports that she has been going to the casinos quite regularly over the past 2 years, gambling on baccarat and jackpot machines. She usually spends a few hundred dollars each time at the casino although she sometimes spends up to 2 thousand dollars. She mentions that she could spend up to half a day gambling at the casinos. Usually, she would spend a few hours at the slot machines, followed by several hours on the baccarat table. She typically plays a few hundred games at the slot machines in 2–3 hours whilst the amount of plays at the baccarat table would depend on how much money she has left after playing the slot machines. She feels thrilled when she wins huge amounts of money at the casino and says that it makes her feel very happy and she also reports a significant amount of cravings to gamble whenever her mood is low. She feels that she is able to stop gambling once she loses a certain amount of money in a day and she sets it as 500 dollars as her stop loss amount. Usually, she is able to keep to this stop loss amount.

What is the severity of her addiction?

For Susan's case, I would define pleasure as 4 as she does experience significant pleasure when she wins big at the casino. I would define urge as 4 as well as she does report significant amount of cravings to gamble when her mood is low. With regards to speed of her gambling, it appears that she does gamble  fairly rapidly at the slot machines, with one game every few minutes or so. Hence, I would quantify the speed of her gambling as 4 as well. With regards to her control over her gambling, I would quantify it as 3 as although she is able to keep to the stop loss of amount of 500 dollars, she can sometimes spend up to 2 thousand dollars gambling, so this is not consistent and her control can be described as moderate as best.

Earlier in the first chapter, we said that as pleasure goes down, the urge goes up as the user moves from the impulsive stage to the compulsive stage. For the second scenario, both pleasure and urge are at 4 in terms of severity and it is true that sometimes both are still at this high level during the intermediate stages of the illness. Hence it can be understood that addiction is a fairly dynamic process and there are really no absolutes in terms of how the trajectory of the illness moves over time.

In terms of addiction severity, therefore it would be

$$\text{Addiction severity} = (4 + 4) \times 4^2/3 = 42.7$$

This would therefore indicate a moderate severity of addiction. We can again track this severity over time and monitor on the variables to see the progression. Such is the utility of this equation to be able to track dynamically the changes that occur in Susan's condition with treatment.

QUIZ TIME 10:

1. What does McNaughton's principles state?

    a) For a defence of insanity, a person must not know the nature of his actions or if he did, he knew what he was doing was wrong

    b) For a defence of insanity, a person must not know the nature of his actions or if he did, he did not know what he was doing was wrong

    c) For a defence of insanity, a person must know the nature of his actions, but not what he was doing was wrong

    d) For a defence of insanity, a person must know the nature of his actions and what he was doing was wrong

2. Which regulation in Singapore requires medical practitioners to report someone suspected of a drug addiction to the authorities?

   a) MDR-19

   b) MDR-16

   c) MDR-18

   d) MDR-20

3. Drugs are classified into how many classes in the misuse of drugs Act of Singapore?

   a) 3

   b) 4

   c) 5

   d) 6

11

ALCOHOL AND THE BODY

Guest chapter by Dr Sara Cheo

This guest chapter is written by Dr Sara Cheo, a gastroenterologist, who has treated patients suffering from physical ailments secondary to the use of alcohol. The reason why alcohol was chosen was because of its easy availability as a legal substance and it's effects on public health at a population level due to this easy availability. Beyond addiction, very often the effects of the substances affects the physical health of the users and we will use alcohol as an example of what can happen to the physical health of an individual when such substances are consumed.

Effects of Alcohol on Your Body

Alcohol can affect the body in various ways. Most of the deleterious effects of alcohol are associated with a consumption history higher than what is considered safe in health guidelines. However, the research so far has been hampered in that there are no existing long term randomized trials (what researchers consider as the gold standard quality of research) of the effects of long term alcohol use. However, there is sufficient evidence to raise concern about the effects of alcohol on the human body.

What is the "safe amount of alcohol" to drink?

This question does not have a straightforward answer. Most guidelines recommend at most no more than 2 drinks a day for males, and no more than 1 drink a day for females. The National Institute on Alcohol Abuse and Alcoholism (NIAAA) in the United States states that for males under the age of 65, drinking more than 14 standard drinks per week or more than 4 drinks on any day is risky alcohol use and raises the risk for health consequences[1]. For females or males aged 65 and older, risky alcohol use would be more than 7 standard drinks per week or more than 3 drinks on any day[1]. The different guidelines based on gender are due to factors such as differences in the way the body processes alcohol in males versus females, and differences in the average body size between the genders.

However, different countries define a standard drink differently. In Singapore, 1 standard drink would be equivalent to 330 mL of regular beer, or 100 mL of wine (half a glass), or 1 shot (30mL) of hard liquor[2].

For some people, drinking any alcohol at all may be harmful. These include pregnant women, patients with underlying liver problems and/or who are on certain medications, people whose job requires them to work with heavy machinery or equipment, and so on. Some experts recommend that the best and safest choice would be no alcohol at all[3].

There is also less awareness about the harms of binge drinking. People who binge drink may not drink all the time, but they drink a lot of alcohol in a short time, for example, 5 or more drinks for males in 2 hours.

What are signs that you have a problem with drinking?
There are several tools or questionaires that have been used to test quickly if someone has signs of problems with their alcohol use. A simple and easy way is by asking the CAGE questions. Essentially CAGE stands for felt you should Cut down on drinking, Annoyance after being criticized on drinking, felt Guilty about drinking and taken an Eye-opener.[4]

A single "yes" response is considered as a positive result.

A more detailed test would be the Alcohol Use Disorders Identification Test (AUDIT), which asks 10 questions and scores the answers accordingly. There are also several variations of this test. AUDIT is usually used by general practitioners as a more precise screening tool compared to CAGE.

Effects of Alcohol on the Body

1) Alcohol poisoning

Alcohol poisoning can occur when someone drinks far too much alcohol, and this can be life-threatening. For example, a person with alcohol poisoning could stop breathing or choke on their own vomit. Alcohol poisoning is a medical emergency, and persons suffering from this should have an ambulance called to bring them to hospital immediately.

2) Cancer

Alcohol has been classified by the World Health Organization (WHO) as a class 1 carcinogen, meaning that there is sufficient evidence to prove that this substance causes cancer in humans[5]. The cancers that alcohol has been associated with include breast, mouth, larynx and pharynx cancer, and cancers of the digestive tract, including esophageal, liver, pancreatic, and colorectal cancer. While heavy drinking is certainly worse, some cancers have been found to occur more commonly even with just a moderate consumption of alcohol. For example, the risk of breast cancer is increased by drinking just 1 to 2 drinks a day[6]. Certain other factors may worsen this risk; for example, patients who smoke and drink are at a significantly higher risk of developing head and neck cancer[7].

Cardiovascular (Heart and Stroke) Problems

Heavy drinking increases the risk of developing atrial fibrillation, which is an abnormal heart rhythm. Heavy alcohol consumption also increases the risk of high blood pressure and stroke. Long term heavy drinking also can lead to heart failure. While there have been some studies that suggest that light to moderate consumption of alcohol can protect against coronary artery disease[8], there have also been other studies challenging this benefit. For example, a study found that even light to moderate alcohol consumption has been associated with higher rates of stroke, heart failure, and non-heart attack related cardiovascular mortality[9]. Neither is there clear evidence that drinking wine is better for the heart than other forms of alcohol[10]. Considering all the known problems associated with drinking alcohol, it would not be advisable to consume alcohol for the sole purpose of cardiovascular risk reduction.

Alcoholic Liver Disease

Alcoholic liver disease can manifest in a few ways- as alcoholic hepatitis, alcohol related fatty liver disease, cirrhosis and its complications, and hepatocellular carcinoma.

Patients with alcoholic hepatitis may present with symptoms such as jaundice (yellowing of the eyes and/or skin and tea-coloured urine), poor appetite, fever, and pain or discomfort over the right upper abdomen. The prognosis of alcoholic hepatitis varies, but patients with severe alcoholic hepatitis have a mortality rate as high as 45 percent at one month from diagnosis, with death occurring due to liver failure, gastrointestinal bleeding, and infection (sepsis)[11]. The majority of patients who develop alcoholic hepatitis have a history of heavy alcohol use of more than 100 g per day for two or more decades[12].

Cirrhosis means irreversible scarring of the liver. This can manifest as bleeding in the digestive tract, swelling in the abdomen and legs, hepatic encephalopathy (confusion or change in the mental state), and is associated with an increased risk of hepatocellular carcinoma (liver cancer).

For patients with cirrhosis, they may have symptoms such as jaundice, their tummy and their legs may look distended from fluid (ascites), and they may have muscle wasting from malnutrition. They may also be confused or have changes in their mental state from hepatic encephalopathy. However, in early cirrhosis, patients may not have any noticeable symptoms at all. The prognosis of patients with cirrhosis varies greatly based on the stage of cirrhosis. In general, patients with early cirrhosis from any cause have a median survival of > 12 years[13]. However, patients who have developed complications of cirrhosis (such as ascites, hepatic encephalopathy, hepatocellular carcinoma, and so on) are considered to have "decompensated" cirrhosis and have a much worse prognosis than those with early or "compensated" cirrhosis. The median survival was found to be 6 months or less in those patients with decompensated cirrhosis and a Child-Pugh score of 12 or more or a Model for End-stage Liver Disease (MELD) score of 21 or more[14].

Obesity and excess body weight is associated with an increased risk of alcoholic liver disease. If patients have underlying other liver conditions such as chronic viral hepatitis, they are also more likely to develop advanced liver disease.

It is unclear exactly how much alcohol leads to an increase in hepatocellular carcinoma (HCC), although many studies have linked alcohol intake specifically to a higher risk of HCC[15].

Pancreatitis

Pancreatitis is the inflammation of the pancreas, an organ in the body involved with digestion. Patients with acute pancreatitis usually have severe abdominal pain, which often requires hospitalization for monitoring and pain management. Over time, patients can also develop chronic pancreatitis, which is irreversible. Patients with chronic pancreatitis usually have problems digesting their food properly, and can develop malnutrition and vitamin deficiencies. They also often develop diabetes as a result.

Gastritis and Esophagitis

Alcohol can contribute to developing gastritis (inflammation of the stomach) and esophagitis (inflammation of the esophagus or food pipe). Even patients who do not have problems controlling their alcohol intake should avoid alcohol if they are suffering from gastritis and esophagitis.

Osteoporosis

People who drink heavily are more likely to have osteoporosis, a condition in which bones are more brittle. Patients with osteoporosis have an increased risk of fractures.

Gout

Drinking alcohol can increase the risk of developing gout, and can also triggers gout attacks in patients with existing gout.

Blood Abnormalities

Alcohol has several known effects on the blood system, including causing low haemoglobin counts (anaemia), low platelet counts (thrombocytopenia), low white cell counts (leucopenia), and bone marrow abnormalities. It is known to cause direct toxic effects on the production of red blood cells in the bone marrow. Several of its effects on the blood are also as a result of its effects on other parts of the body. For example, alcoholic liver disease can contribute to longer bleeding times and difficulty in the blood clotting. Patients may bruise easily and injuries may bleed more than usual.

Brain and Nerve Damage, Effect on Mental Health

Drinking affects judgement, decision making and coordination. As such, there is a higher risk of accidents such as accidental injuries, traffic accidents, drowning, and suicide. Alcohol consumption also increase the risk of violence. Long term heavy drinking can affect thinking and memory, and lead to dementia and other chronic degenerative brain diseases. It can also lead to muscle weakness, nerve damage and problems with coordination.

Sexual Dysfunction

Excessive drinking is related to sexual dysfunction, especially male impotency.

Pregnancy Complications

Alcohol consumption is associated with an increased risk of pregnancy loss or stillbirth. Drinking during pregnancy is also linked with causing a condition called fetal alcohol spectrum disorder in babies, which causes low birth weight, smaller heads, growth and developmental problems and delays, and brain damage. Babies whose mothers drank alcohol while pregnant are also more likely to develop behavioural and social problems when they become older. No amount of alcohol has been found to be safe during pregnancy[16], and as such, doctors advise complete alcohol avoidance during pregnancy[16]. If you want to get pregnant, you should stop drinking alcohol before you even start trying for pregnancy, especially as you may not know you are pregnant in the first few weeks of pregnancy.

Alcohol Withdrawal and Delirium Tremens

When people who have been drinking for a long time try to cut back on drinking, they may develop symptoms from alcohol withdrawal. Symptoms can start as soon as 6 hours, or within 24 hours after stopping drinking[17]. Mild symptoms of withdrawal include having trouble sleeping, tremors, anxiety, nausea, headaches, sweating, and having palpitations. More serious symptoms include seizures, hallucinations which can be visual, auditory, or even tactile (you feel things that are not there-for example complaints of feeling like ants crawling all over your body). The most severe form of this syndrome would be delirium tremens, which can even lead to death. As such, patients who have been drinking heavily and want to cut back should try to do so under the supervision of a medical professional. Medical professionals often use the CIWA Alcohol Withdrawal Scale to objectively assess and manage medical intervention for patients undergoing alcohol withdrawal. The Scale uses symptoms such as nausea and vomiting, tremors, sweating, anxiety, agitation, tactile disturbances, auditory disturbances, visual disturbances, headaches, and disorientation or confusion to grade the severity of alcohol withdrawal. Mild symptoms may be treated symptomatically at home, but some patients may require observation or treatment at a healthcare facility to safely withdraw from alcohol. If you suspect someone is having delirium tremens, this is a medical emergency. Call an ambulance to bring them to hospital immediately.

References

1. National Institute on Alcohol Abuse and Alcoholism. Helping patient who drink too much: A clinician's guide. NIH Publication no. 05-3769, Bethesda, MD 2005.

2. HealthHub. https://www.healthhub.sg/live-healthy/alcohol-and-health-set-your-drinking-limits. Accessed 10 Jan 2025.

3. Rock CL et al. American Cancer Society guideline for diet and physical activity for cancer prevention. CA Cancer J Clin. 2020; 70 (4): 245.

4. Ewing JA. Detecting alcoholism. The CAGE questionnaire. JAMA. 1984 Oct 12;252(14):1905–7.

5. World Health Organization. https://monographs.iarc.who.int/agents-classified-by-the-iarc/. Accessed 12 Jan 2025.

6. Cao Y et al. Light to moderate intake of alcohol, drinking patterns, and risk of cancer: result from two prospective US cohort studies. BMJ. 2015 Aug 18; 351: h4238.

7. Choi SY et al. Effect of cigarette smoking and alcohol consumption in the aetiology of cancer of the oral cavity, pharynx and larynx. Int J Epidemiol. 1991; 20 (4): 878.

8. Ronksley PE et al. Association of alcohol consumption with selected cardiovascular disease outcomes: a systematic review and meta-analysis. BMJ. 2011; 342: d671.

9. Wood AM et al. Risk thresholds for alcohol consumption: combined analysis of individual-participant data for 599 912 current drinkers in 83 prospective studies. Lancet. 2018; 391 (10129): 1513.

10. Mukamal KJ et al. Roles of drinking pattern and type of alcohol consumed in coronary heart disease in men. NEJM. 2003; 348 (2): 109

11. Yu CH et al. Early mortality of alcoholic hepatitis: a review of data from placebo-controlled clinical trials. World J Gastroenterol. 2010 May; 16 (19): 2435.

12. Mendenhall CL et al. A study of oral nutritional support with oxandrolone in malnourished patients with alcoholic hepatitis: results of a Department of Veterans Affairs cooperative study. Hepatology. 1993; 17 (4): 564.

13. D'Amico G et al. Natural history and prognostic indicators of survival in cirrhosis: a systematic review of 118 studies. J Hepatol. 2006; 44 (1): 217.

14. Salpeter SR et al. Systematic review of noncancer presentations with a median survival of 6 months or less. Am J Med. 2012 May; 125 (5): 512.

15. Mancebo A et al. Annual incidence of hepatocellular carcinoma among patients with alcoholic cirrhosis and identification of risk groups. Clin Gastroenterol Hepatol. 2013; 11 (1): 95.

16. Kesmodel US et al. Are Low-to-Moderate Average Alcohol Consumption and Isolated Episodes of Binge Drinking in Early Pregnancy Associated with Facial Features Related to Fetal Alcohol Syndrome in 5-Year-Old Children? Alcohol Clin Exp Res. 2019; 43 (6): 1199.

17. Turner RC et al. Alcohol withdrawal syndromes: a review of pathophysiology, clinical presentation, and treatment. J Gen Intern Med. 1989; 4(5): 432.

QUIZ TIME 11:

1. Which of the following cancers have **not** been associated with heavy alcohol consumption?

    A. Breast

    B. Kidney

    C. Colorectal

    D. Pharynx

2. How much alcohol is safe to drink in pregnancy?

    A. One glass of wine per day

    B. One can of beer per day

    C. Any amount is safe as long as you drink responsibly

    D. No amount of alcohol has been found to be safe

3. Which of the symptom below is **not** a sign of delirium tremens?

    A. Increased appetite

    B. Tremors

    C. Agitation

    D. Sweating

ANSWERS TO QUIZZES:

Chapter 1:

1. a

2. c

3. b

Chapter 2:

1. c

2. a

3. d

Chapter 3:

    1. a

    2. a

    3. d

Chapter 4:

    1. d

    2. c

    3. a

Chapter 5:

    1. b

    2. d

    3. c

 **CHAPTER 11**

Chapter 6:

    1. a

    2. c

    3. b

Chapter 7:

    1. a

    2. d

    3. d

Chapter 8:

    1. b

    2. a

    3. d

Chapter 9:

    1. a

    2. d

    3. d

Chapter 10:

    1. b

    2. a

    3. a

Chapter 11:

    1. b

    2. d

    3. a

INDEX

abstinence, 25, 108
    abstinent, 61
acetaldehyde, 50
acetylcholine, 48
    receptors, 44
acute detoxification, 12
addiction counsellors, 9
addiction equation, 15, 21, 22, 42, 65, 163
addiction progresses, 3, 4
addictions, 2, 37
addictiveness, 3
addictive personality, 103
adverse childhood experiences, 42, 62
alcohol, 33, 44
    dependence, 50
alcoholics anonymous (AA), 12, 24, 145, 146
alcoholic liver disease, 179
alcohol poisoning, 178
alcohol use disorder, 21, 22, 24, 25
algorithm, 103

amygdala, 10, 46, 47, 59
antidepressants, 33
artificial intelligence, 76
attention deficit hyperactivity disorder (ADHD), 42, 92, 104
AUDIT, 178
automatic thoughts, 117, 118
avatars, 81
aversion, 11
    therapy, 116
aversive stimulus, 50

barbiturates, 44
basal drives, 98
basal ganglia, 47
behavioural addiction, 29, 30, 36, 37, 116
benzodiazepines, 32, 33, 44, 108
binge drinking, 114, 115, 133
biological impulses, 11
biorhythms, 11
bipolar disorder, 33

 INDEX

blackouts, 27
Blood Abnormalities, 182
Brain and Nerve Damage, Effect
   on Mental Health, 182
bupropion, 33, 116

CAGE, 177
Cancer, 178
cannabis, 28, 43
Cardiovascular (Heart and
   Stroke) Problems, 179
casinos, 24
CBT, 52, 119, 120
Central Narcotics Bureau, 62,
   150, 158
charting, 12
chemical properties, 11
chronic brain disease, 58
chronic condition, 58
chronic illness, 59, 71
Classical Conditioning, 49, 51
cocktail, 33
cognitive behavioural
   therapies, 11, 47, 117
cold turkey, 144
community resources, 12, 151
community supports, 145
co-morbid, 37, 42, 126
compensatory mechanisms, 26
competing force, 46, 98
compulsively, 4
compulsiveness, 35, 37

compulsive sexual behavioural
   disorder, 23, 30, 36, 37
computer algorithms, 85
conditioning, 42, 52
control, 2, 5–14, 23, 25, 31, 36,
   66, 112, 113, 117, 164
cough mixture, 43
counselling, 10
cravings, 3, 4, 11–14, 21, 28,
   29, 47, 52, 60, 65
cues, 59
curated, 77, 101
cut down, 25
   cutting down, 23
cyber bullied, 79

decision making, 45
delirium tremens, 24, 183
dependent, 26, 32, 47
depressants, 33
desire, 7
detoxification, 51
   detoxify, 13
detoxification phase, 144
diagnostic criteria, 22
diagnostic manuals, 21
differential disorders, 34
different phases, 12
disinhibition, 24
disulfiram, 50, 53
doom-scrolling, 5, 8
dopamine, 44, 46, 48

dopamine spike, 77
dorsolateral prefrontal cortex, 45
downer, 33
drug laws, 158
drug rehabilitation centre, 12,
    13, 43, 50, 60, 159
DSM-5, 21, 22, 29, 36, 80, 159
DSM-IV, 29
dynamic, 22
        pathway, 48

eating disorder, 34
e-cigarettes, 86, 87
ecstasy, 44
ego-dystonic, 35
ego-syntonic, 35
emotional regulation, 106
empathy, 129
endorphins, 48
environmental, 62
        factors, 42
equation, 9
erectile dysfunction, 83, 84
euphoric, 48
        reaction, 31
        sensations, 10
excitatory impulses, 47
executive functioning, 10

faith-based services, 144
false assurance, 25
fear of missing out, 78, 101

feedback loops, 48
frontal cortex, 45–47, 98
functioning alcoholic, 26

GABA, 48
        receptors, 44
gabapentin, 32
gamblers anonymous, 145
gambling, 29, 76
        disorder, 24, 36
gaming disorder, 29, 37
gastritis and esophagitis, 181
generative AI, 30
genetic, 62
        predisposition, 42
Gout, 182

halfway house, 145, 150
        residential programmes,
        150
hangovers, 27
hazardous, 28
Health Promotion Board, 150
heroin, 3, 12–14, 33, 43, 46, 52,
    60, 99, 100, 108, 114
high, 99
higher cognitive functions, 45
higher cortical functions, 10
highway, 13, 99, 100
hijacked, 46, 48, 129
hippocampus, 10, 46, 59
homeostasis, 32, 33, 107

 INDEX

ICD-11, 21, 29, 36, 37, 80
illusion of control, 24, 25
imbalance, 33, 34
impairment, 30, 31
impairment of function, 25, 26
impulse control disorder, 29, 30, 36
impulsively, 4
index of suspicion, 27
inhalants, 28
inhibitory control, 46–48
initial phases, 3
inpatient, 144
insight, 25
instant gratification, 5, 8
internal balance, 34
internal milieu, 107
interventions, 9
intoxicated, 24, 25, 114
intractable illness, 128
intravenous, 13
intrinsic properties, 3

jackpot machines, 81
judgement, 10, 45

kindling, 105, 116

liking, 4
limbic system, 10, 45
limits, 24
liver failure, 21
LSD, 44

manipulate, 114
mastery, 11
masturbating, 23
mathematical formula, 2
McNaughton's Rules, 160
MDR-19, 158
medical detoxification, 50
medications, 10–12, 58, 116
meditation, 107
memory, 27
mesolimbic pathways, 10
Methamphetamine, 29, 33
milestones, 60
mindfulness, 11, 52, 105–108
minimize, 29
Ministry of Education, 150
mirtazapine, 33
moral problem, 58
motivational interviewing, 47, 129, 131, 133
motor system, 10

Naltrexone, 114–116
narcotics anonymous (NA), 12, 24, 145, 146
National Council on Problem Gambling, 150
negative affective symptoms, 10
negative automatic thoughts, 120
negative emotions, 27
negative reinforcement, 49, 50
negative sensations, 4

neurobiological process, 5, 10
neuroplasticity, 92
nicotine, 44
NMDA, 48
non-confrontational, 133
nucleus accumbens, 45, 46

obsessive compulsive disorder
   (OCD), 34, 35
occupational therapy, 144
online bullying, 79
online gambling, 81, 84
online multiplayer games, 76
operant conditioning, 49
opioid dependence, 3
osteoporosis, 181
outpatient treatments, 144
overdose toxicity, 99
over-kindled, 48

pain, 128
pancreatitis, 181
paraphilic disorders, 37
pathological gambling, 29, 36
Pavlovian conditioning, 51
peers in recovery, 145
peer support, 145
performance, 27
perpetuating, 62, 65
personality problems, 63
pharmacological treatment,
   47
physical dependence, 28

pleasure, 2–4, 7–10, 14, 66,
   112, 113, 164
polysubstance, 33
pornography, 23, 61, 76, 83,
   89
positive feedback, 10
positive reinforcement, 49, 50
powerless, 24
precipitating, 62, 65
precipitating factor, 63
predisposing, 62, 65
pre-frontal cortex, 10, 47
pregabalin, 32
pregnancy complications, 183
preoccupied, 23
primal drives, 10
primary care providers, 144
primary motor cortex, 45
prison, 43
progress, 15
prophylactic, 34
protective, 65
   factors, 62
pruning, 61
psychiatric opinion, 160
psychiatrists, 9
psychoeducation, 148
   groups, 150
psychosocial, 144
   dependence, 31
   pain, 127
   theories, 49
   therapies, 47

 INDEX

impairment, 21
measures, 12
psychostimulants, 33, 34
psychotropics, 33
punishment, 49, 50

quick fixes, 108

rapid reinstatement, 24
recommended guidelines, 27
recovery, 58, 61–63, 65, 67,
    149
recovery journey, 60
recovery stories, 127
regulatory control, 98
rehabilitation, 149
rehabilitation phase, 12, 144
re-kindles, 129
relapse, 4, 24, 58, 59, 62, 128,
    131, 149
remission, 58, 59, 61
remission rates, 128
residential programmes, 149
residential treatment
    programme, 145
resilience, 59
rewarding stimulus, 10
reward pathway, 5, 34, 44, 46,
    48, 58, 59, 129
rewards, 49
Risk Factors, 42

sadomasochism, 83
Salience, 23, 26, 31, 81

schemas, 118–120
sedation, 32
sedative hypnotics, 32
seek treatment, 4
Selective Serotonin Reuptake
    Inhibitors, 116
self-gratification, 102
self-medication, 34
self-reinforcing, 30
septic emboli, 100
sequential monitoring, 9
serotonin, 48
serotonin receptors, 44
severity, 5, 12, 21
severity of an Addiction, 3
Sex and Love Addicts
    Anonymous, 145
sexual deviancy, 37
Sexual Dysfunction, 182
sexual thoughts, 23
Sinclair method, 114, 115
sleeping pills, 43
slip, 61, 149
slippery slope, 24, 25, 62, 128,
    163
social deprivation, 44
social learning theory, 52
social media, 5, 6, 8, 30, 38, 76,
    77, 80, 81, 89, 92, 101
social problem, 44
social service agencies, 145,
    150
specialist treatment service,
    144

speed, 2, 5–10, 14, 66, 98, 112,
  164
stages of change, 22
standard drinks, 176
stigma, 29, 126, 151
stimulants, 33
stranglehold, 26
subcortical structures, 46
substance use disorder, 3
subutex, 60, 100
surf, 77
symptoms, 4

telescoping, 89, 91
therapists, 9
therapy, 10–12, 58, 116
thermostat, 34
token economy, 49
tolerance, 10, 21, 28, 32
transtheoretical model, 129,
  147
treatment, 28

treatment outcomes, 25
triggers, 11
12-step, 146

underpinnings, 10
unmask, 63
upstream work, 62, 151
urge, 2–5, 7–10, 12, 23, 52, 60,
  66, 112, 113, 164

vaping, 86
varenicline, 117
ventral tegmental area, 45, 46
virtual communities, 81
voyeuristic behaviour, 37

withdrawal, 4, 10, 35, 144
    symptoms, 3, 4, 7, 11–14,
      28, 50, 65

Z-drugs, 32

www.ingramcontent.com/pod-product-compliance
Lightning Source LLC
Chambersburg PA
CBHW061628250726
48659CB00004B/1119